THE YOUNG
RIDER

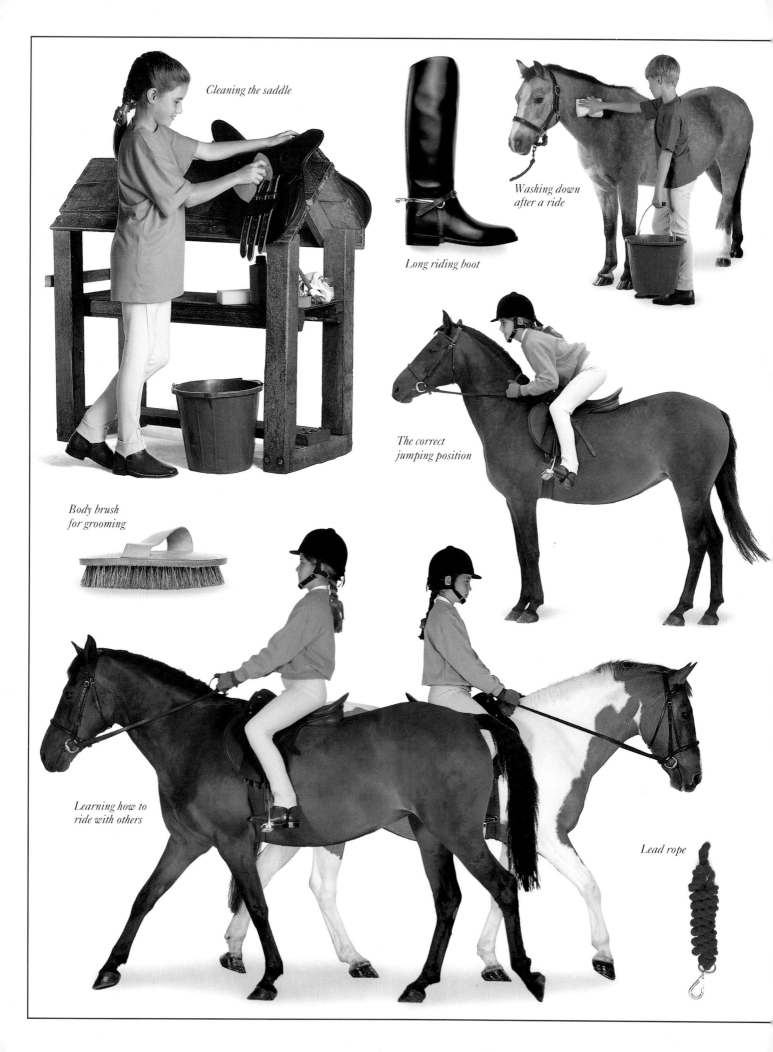

Cleaning the saddle

Long riding boot

Washing down after a ride

The correct jumping position

Body brush for grooming

Learning how to ride with others

Lead rope

*Hand signals
for road riding*

THE YOUNG RIDER

Mane comb

*Quick-release
knot*

LUCINDA GREEN

*Exercises in
the saddle*

Riding clothes

*Velvet-covered
hard hat*

Halter

DORLING KINDERSLEY, INC.
NEW YORK

A DORLING KINDERSLEY BOOK

Project editor Christiane Gunzi   **Art editor** Floyd Sayers

Equestrian consultant Gig Lees

Special photography Ray Moller

Editorial assistance Jill Somerscales

Production Jayne Wood

Managing editor Sophie Mitchell
Managing art editor Miranda Kennedy

U. S. editor B. Alison Weir

The young riders
Nathalie Turton, Marissa Deardon,
Phillippa Sayers, Christophe de Gruben

Photographed at
Wellington Riding, Heckfield, Hampshire, England

First American Edition, 1993
2 4 6 8 10 9 7 5 3 1

Published in the United States by
Dorling Kindersley, Inc., 232 Madison Avenue
New York, New York 10016

ISBN 1-56458-320-1
CIP data is available.

Color reproduction by Colourscan, Singapore
Printed and bound in Italy by Arnoldo Mondadori

 # Contents

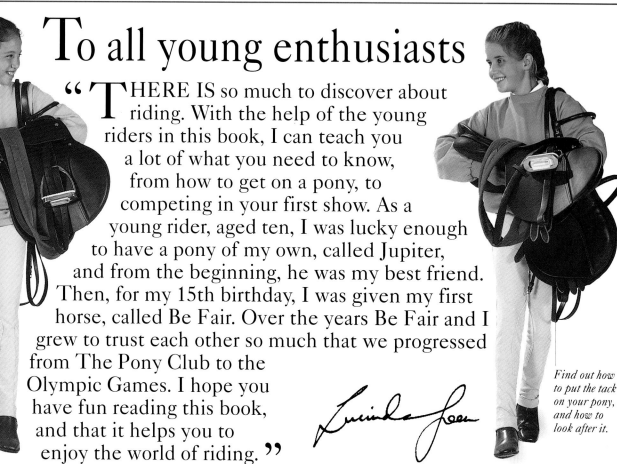

To all young enthusiasts

"THERE IS so much to discover about riding. With the help of the young riders in this book, I can teach you a lot of what you need to know, from how to get on a pony, to competing in your first show. As a young rider, aged ten, I was lucky enough to have a pony of my own, called Jupiter, and from the beginning, he was my best friend. Then, for my 15th birthday, I was given my first horse, called Be Fair. Over the years Be Fair and I grew to trust each other so much that we progressed from The Pony Club to the Olympic Games. I hope you have fun reading this book, and that it helps you to enjoy the world of riding."

Find out how to put the tack on your pony, and how to look after it.

As you learn to ride, your pony will become your friend.

Learn how to control your pony, so that you are always confident in the saddle.

Discover how to groom your pony, so that it is always neat.

Find out what a pony eats, so that you will never feed your pony anything harmful.

Never be afraid to ask for a helping hand while you are learning.

See how exciting it is to learn to trot, canter, and jump.

All about riding

P EOPLE AND horses have lived together for a very long time. Thousands of years before the invention of machines, people tamed wild horses so that they could ride them when they hunted for food. Gradually, people began to use horses as a form of transportation, and later, for pulling plows and carts. During the last few hundred years, horses have become so highly trained that today, they take part in all kinds of activities, from pony club shows to Olympic-level dressage performances.

The horse family

Over thousands of years, horses have developed from animals the size of dogs to the many kinds of horses and ponies that we know today. Your first lessons will be on a pony. As you grow, and as your riding improves, you will progress to larger ponies, then possibly, a horse.

The Shetland pony is one of the smallest breeds, and it is popular as a first pony.

The Clydesdale is a type of draft horse. These large, strong horses are used for pulling farm machinery and heavy carts.

All of today's purebred horses developed from this ancient breed, called the Arabian. These horses are physically tough, and they are also very beautiful.

The horse that I am riding here has been trained as an "eventer." This means that it must learn to do dressage, show jumping, and cross-country to a high standard.

This Lipizzan horse has been trained to perform high school movements at the famous Spanish Riding School of Vienna, in Austria.

Riding today

Today, horses are often bred and trained for a particular sport, such as racing, dressage, or polo. The ponies that children ride are usually trained to be "good all-arounders." This means that they are taught to do all sorts of activities, including riding, jumping, and games.

Choosing a riding school

WHEN YOU FIRST start riding, your local 4-H club will probably be able to give you the address of a good riding school. Then, if you go to look at the school, make sure that it is approved by a recognized organization, such as the Horsemanship Safety Association. A good school is neat and tidy, and its ponies look content and well cared for. The people who work at the riding school should be friendly, and all the riders should be wearing crash helmets. Ask if there is an enclosed area such as an arena, or an indoor school, where you can have your first lessons safely. Once you have chosen a school, book a lesson. If you have one or two friends who also want to learn to ride, it may give you confidence to share your first lessons with them.

At the riding school

When you arrive at the riding school, your instructor will find you a crash helmet that fits. Then you will probably go to meet your pony, and you may learn to groom and tack it up. Your instructor will explain what will happen in your first lesson. Try not to worry if it feels like your first time on a bicycle. You will soon relax, make new friends, and have great fun.

The stables
These should be tidy and well looked after, with safety bolts and hinges on the stable doors.

The paddocks
If all the ponies are turned out together, there should be enough grass and space. The pasture should have safe fencing and no litter.

Once you have a suitable hat and footwear, you are ready for a lesson.

A pony of your own

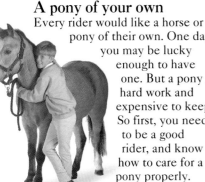

Every rider would like a horse or pony of their own. One day you may be lucky enough to have one. But a pony is hard work and expensive to keep. So first, you need to be a good rider, and know how to care for a pony properly.

The indoor school

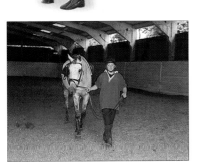

If you are having a lesson in rainy weather, it is useful if there is an indoor arena.

The tack room

The tack should be clean, and the tack room should be tidy.

You may not be sure how to communicate with your pony at first, but it will soon understand your wishes.

This pony is very calm and gentle, so it is perfect for a beginner.

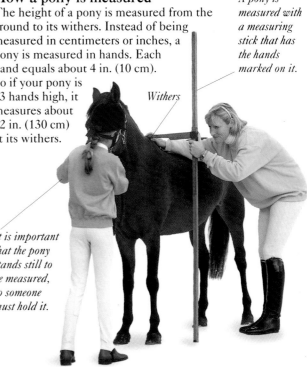

The right pony for you

Your instructor will choose a quiet pony that is suitable for a beginner. Ponies like this are sometimes called "bomb proof," because they are so calm. Your pony should also be just the right size for your height.

When you are sitting on the pony, with your feet in the stirrups, your foot should come to about here.

The muck heap

A neatly stacked muck heap is a sure sign of a good riding school.

How a pony is measured

The height of a pony is measured from the ground to its withers. Instead of being measured in centimeters or inches, a pony is measured in hands. Each hand equals about 4 in. (10 cm). So if your pony is 13 hands high, it measures about 52 in. (130 cm) at its withers.

A pony is measured with a measuring stick that has the hands marked on it.

Withers

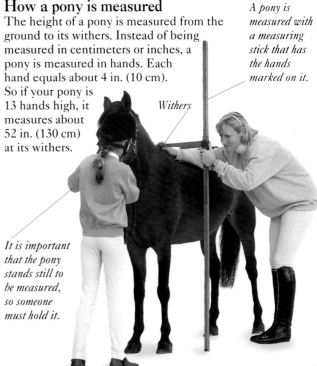

It is important that the pony stands still to be measured, so someone must hold it.

The fire extinguishers

Fire extinguishers should be easy to see, and in good working order.

All about ponies

THERE ARE ALL sorts of things to discover about your pony. Its color and markings each have a special name, and there are unusual names for the different parts of its body. You can also find out some interesting facts about pony breeds and pony behavior. Most horses and ponies are friendly if you treat them kindly. They enjoy getting attention, and will soon learn to recognize you as a friend. You may be a little unsure of a pony at first, but you will quickly learn not to be afraid. As you begin to make friends with your pony, make sure that you do not give it too many treats. If you feed a pony every time that you meet, it will start to expect a treat, and may try to nip you when you do not feed it.

Making friends
Speak to the pony gently, as if it is a friend. If you feed it a treat, hold your hand out flat, keeping your thumb out of the way. Remember that ponies are large, heavy animals, and some can be nervous. If you are noisy, you may frighten your pony, and it could jump and accidentally hurt you. So be kind and careful when you are with ponies.

The points of a pony
The different parts of the body, such as the muzzle, withers, and hoof, are called the points. Together, all these points make up the overall shape, which is called the conformation. It is useful to learn some of these words so that you will be able to understand when your riding instructor mentions them during your lessons.

As a pony grows older, the shape of its teeth change. This is one way to tell its age.

Making faces
Sometimes a pony reacts to an unusual smell or taste by curling its upper lip. This kind of behavior is called "flehmen."

Pony behavior
If you learn a little about how ponies behave with each other, you will be able to understand your pony better. In a group of wild ponies, one of the older ponies will usually be the boss over the others. Tame ponies still behave in this way when they are turned out together. Here one pony is keeping another in its place.

Poll · Mane · Crest · Withers · Back · Forelock · Forehead · Cheekbone · Nose · Nostril · Muzzle · Chin groove · Throat · Jugular groove · Shoulder · Breast · Forearm · Elbow · Belly · Knee · Chestnut · Cannon bone · Pastern · Ergot · Coronet

Ears forward show that this pony is listening and interested.

Ears back show that this pony is less alert and uninterested.

All about ears
A pony's ears are constantly moving backward and forward to listen to sounds in front and behind. If a pony is angry, both its ears are flat back, and the whites of its eyes show.

Learning about colors

A pony may be white, but it is called a gray. If its coat is freckled, it is a "fleabitten" gray. Black and white ponies are known as pintos. If your pony has black, brown, or chestnut hair mixed with white, it is called a blue or a strawberry roan. Here are some of the other colors that you may see at the stables. Try to remember the names, as they will help you to recognize the ponies that you meet.

Bay

Dapple gray

Chestnut

Dun

Pinto

Palomino

All about hooves

A pony's hooves are extremely strong. Whenever the pony moves, the hoof wall takes the whole weight of the body.

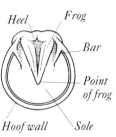

Heel

Frog

Bar

Point of frog

Hoof wall

Sole

Each hoof consists of three main parts. These are called the sole, the hoof wall, and the frog. There are several other parts, too, which you can see here.

Learning about markings

All the different markings on a pony's legs, body, and face have a name. If you learn these, you will find it easier to spot the difference between two ponies that are the same color at a distance. Horses and ponies sometimes have a patch of white on their face, such as a star, a stripe, or a blaze. A very small splash of white on the tip of the muzzle is called a snip.

Dorsal stripe

Stocking

Sock

White coronet

Dorsal stripe

A black line all the way along a pony's spine is called a "dorsal stripe."

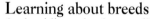

Star

Stripe

Blaze

Loins

Croup

Dock

Tail

Thigh

Flank

Stifle

Hock joint

Tendons

Shank

Heel

Fetlock joint

Hoof

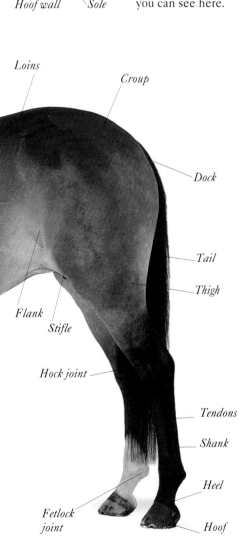

Welsh Ponies are tough, and came originally from the mountains of Wales.

Learning about breeds

At the riding school, you will probably see many different types of ponies. These have all developed from the native breeds of pony which have lived on Earth for thousands of years. The Arab horse is probably the oldest breed of all. Many of the ponies that people ride today are a mixture of several breeds, and they are called "crossbreeds."

Exmoor Ponies have lived in the wild on cold English moorlands since before the Ice Age.

Riding ponies are crossbred, that is, a mixture of breeds such as Welsh and Arabian.

What a rider wears

RIDERS NEED to wear special clothing for safety and comfort. For everyday riding, you can wear whatever you choose, as long as you have the correct hat and a pair of riding boots, or suitable shoes. But if you take part in a show, you will need more formal clothes so that you look professional. The most important piece of equipment is your riding hat, which protects your head if you fall off the pony. The hat must fit your head properly, and be comfortable enough for you to wear every moment that you are riding.

If your hair is long, tie it back or wear a hairnet.

You can wear a colorful helmet cover to protect it.

A loose sweater or sweatshirt is comfortable for everyday riding.

Riding in the rain
When you ride in rainy weather, a waterproof riding coat or a slicker will help keep you warm and dry. If it rains very heavily, you will probably find that you are wet anyway. But this is all part of riding.

Hard hats and helmets
There are two types of riding hat. A hard hat or hunt cap is covered with velvet, with a peak at the front. A crash helmet, like this one, has no peak. You will probably wear one of these when you start riding. Proper riding hats have a special label inside, which proves that they will protect your head well if you hit it.

Make sure that these straps are fastened tightly so that your helmet stays in place.

This chin cup helps keep the helmet in position.

Extra padding on the jodhpurs stops your legs from rubbing against the saddle.

It is best to wear ankle-high jodhpur boots, like these. They protect your ankles, and have no buckles or laces to get caught in the stirrups.

Boots
It is important to wear the correct boots for riding. These have a heel to stop your foot from slipping through the stirrup. Jodhpur boots are ankle-high and are made of leather.

Gloves
The correct gloves to wear are proper riding gloves, made of cotton, nylon, or wool. They have a special surface that helps you grip the reins. You can also wear leather gloves, but these may become slippery if they get wet.

Wool riding gloves

Leather riding gloves

Cotton riding gloves

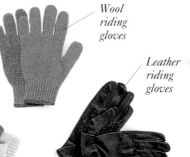

What to wear for everyday riding
The most comfortable clothes for riding are jodhpurs and a loose-fitting top with long sleeves. Remember to wear your gloves, take your whip, and always fasten your crash helmet properly before you get on the pony.

A hard hat covered with velvet is part of the formal outfit for a dressage test.

If you join a pony club, you can wear a pony club tie.

For any show you will need a white shirt and a tie.

Hunting stock

This special kind of tie is worn over a white shirt for cross-country riding. First you wind it around your neck, on top of your collar, then you tie it up at the front.

A smart black jacket like this one is for wearing on special occasions.

A knob at the top of your crop helps stop it from slipping through your hand.

These breeches end at the ankle. They are for wearing with tall boots.

Riding crop

It is always a good idea to carry a crop when you are riding. But if your crop has a loop at the end, never put your hand through it when you are riding. If you were to fall off, the crop could stick into you.

Jodhpurs stretch so that you can bend your legs easily.

Tall rubber or leather boots are usually worn with breeches.

Body protector

The body protector is a very important part of the equipment for cross-country riding. It is usually worn on top of your other clothes, and protects your body if you fall. Although a body protector may seem rather heavy and hot at first, after a while it will feel more comfortable.

What to wear to a show

If you go to a show, you may need to wear a riding jacket, some beige or white jodhpurs, jodhpur boots, and a velvet-covered hard hat. Remember to polish your boots and brush your hat.

What to wear on formal occasions

On formal occasions or for dressage tests, you may need a black jacket and pony club tie. You can either wear short or tall boots. Adults usually wear tall boots, which are expensive. Short boots look very good on young riders.

Your first lesson

ONE OF THE first things you must learn when you start riding is how to get on and off the pony safely. This is called mounting and dismounting. Before you begin to mount, you need to check that the girth is tight enough so that the saddle does not slide around. Now you can start to mount. Your instructor will make sure that the pony is standing still while you get on. The usual way is to put one foot in the stirrup and to spring up. You can also mount by standing on a mounting block, which makes it easier. An even simpler way is to ask for a leg up. Once you are sitting on the pony, try to relax. It may seem strange at first, but it will soon feel more comfortable.

Checking the stirrups
Before you mount, run both stirrups down to the bottom of the leathers. To make sure that each leather is roughly the right length, put one hand on the buckle and hold the leather against your arm. The stirrup should just reach your armpit.

Tightening the girth
Lift the top flap of the saddle and tighten both of the girth straps evenly. You may need to walk around to the other side of the pony to check that the buckles are level on both sides.

Asking for a leg up
Facing the pony's left side, gather up the reins in your left hand and put your right hand on the saddle. Bend your left leg and ask someone to give you a leg up. As you are pushed up, swing your right leg over the saddle. Once you are in the saddle, feel for each of the stirrups with your feet.

How to mount

The stirrups
Turn the back edge of the stirrup iron toward you, rather than away from you.

The reins
Hold both reins in your left hand, so that your right hand is free to hold on to the saddle.

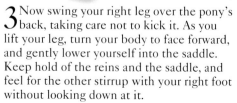

1 Stand with your left shoulder next to the pony's left shoulder, facing the tail. Hold the reins in your left hand, above the mane, in front of the saddle. This helps you keep control of the pony. Then, using your right hand, turn the stirrup iron toward you.

2 Keep hold of the reins with your left hand, and put your left foot into the stirrup. As you do this, turn your body to face the pony's side. Reach up and take hold of the saddle. Then push off the ground lightly with your right foot, so that you are standing in the stirrup on your left foot.

3 Now swing your right leg over the pony's back, taking care not to kick it. As you lift your leg, turn your body to face forward, and gently lower yourself into the saddle. Keep hold of the reins and the saddle, and feel for the other stirrup with your right foot without looking down at it.

How to dismount

Depending on where you live, you will either be taught to take both feet out of the stirrups to dismount, or to keep one foot in the stirrup. Always dismount in the way that your instructor teaches you. If you take both feet out of the stirrups, hold the reins in your left hand, then lean forward and swing your right leg over the pony's back to slide off.

In Australia, a rider dismounts by keeping one foot in the stirrup and stepping off.

In most countries, riders dismount by sliding off, like this.

Adjust the girth

You may need to tighten the girth once you are on the pony, so ask your instructor to help you. Take both reins in your right hand. Then swing your left leg up in front of the saddle flap. Lean down to catch hold of the girth straps with your left hand, and adjust the buckles, one at a time.

Adjust the stirrups

If the stirrups are too short or too long, you can adjust them. Keep your feet in the stirrups when you do this. Take both reins in one hand, then pull the buckle out from under your leg with the other hand. Change the length of the leather, then pull on the inside leather to bring the buckle back to the top.

Holding the reins

Grasp the reins and hold them slightly apart, with your thumbs on top. Make sure the reins are not twisted. Remember that they are attached to the bit, inside the pony's mouth, so never be rough.

Keep your head up and look straight ahead.

Always try to sit upright, with your back straight.

Make sure that you are sitting in the middle of the saddle.

There should be a straight line from your elbows right through to the bit.

Rest the ball of your foot on the stirrup iron, with your toes up and your heels down to help you keep your balance.

4 Once you are sitting in the saddle, there are several things to remember. Hold the reins in both hands, and sit as upright as you can, in the middle of the saddle. Keep your head up, your elbows in, and your heels down. It is important that you feel relaxed, so try not to sit too stiffly. Ask someone to help you adjust the stirrup leathers if they feel too long or too short. Now you are ready to start.

🐎 Take care

As you mount and dismount, try not to prod your pony in the side with your toe.

The first steps of riding

D URING YOUR first few lessons, your instructor will teach you how to control your pony by using "aids," the signals that tell your pony what you want it to do. If the pony is well trained, and if you give the correct signals, you will soon feel in control. The aids that you learn are to slow down, speed up, or turn. Your speed is called the pace, and a change of pace is a transition. It may be a while before you dare to move in the saddle. But as soon as you learn to pat the pony, the happier it will be, and the more you will relax. Try not to pat your pony just before a turn or a transition. You need both hands on the reins for this.

Riding on a lead line
At first, your instructor will lead you on a lunge line. There may be a neck strap to hold as well as reins. If the movement of the pony makes you nervous, hold the neck strap as well as the reins until you are used to it.

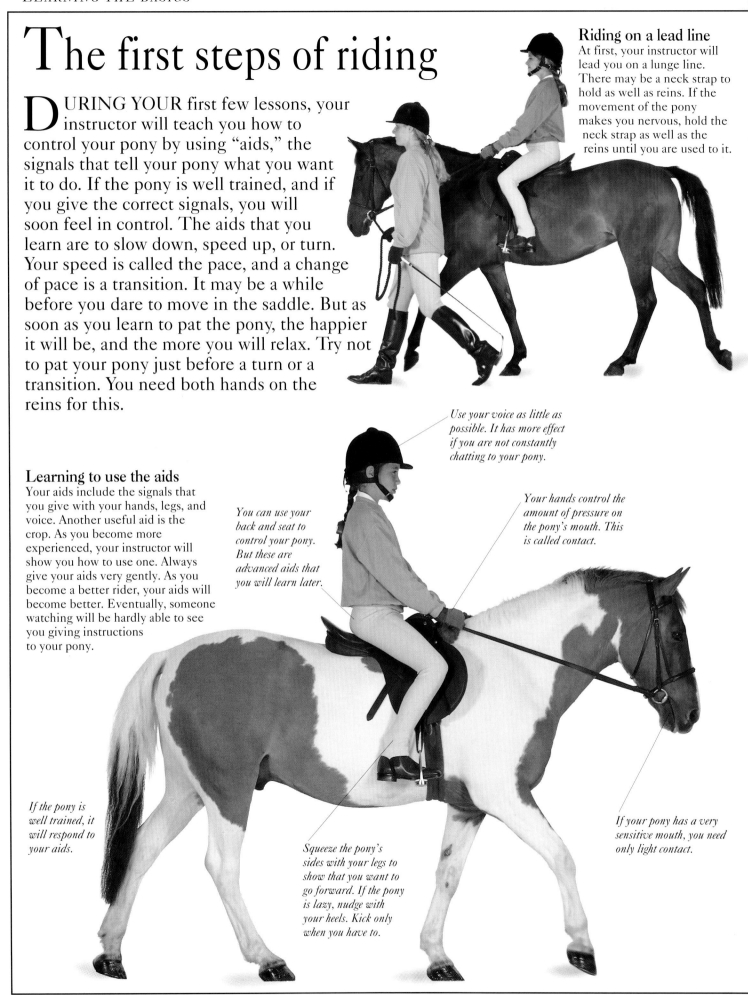

Learning to use the aids
Your aids include the signals that you give with your hands, legs, and voice. Another useful aid is the crop. As you become more experienced, your instructor will show you how to use one. Always give your aids very gently. As you become a better rider, your aids will become better. Eventually, someone watching will be hardly able to see you giving instructions to your pony.

Use your voice as little as possible. It has more effect if you are not constantly chatting to your pony.

You can use your back and seat to control your pony. But these are advanced aids that you will learn later.

Your hands control the amount of pressure on the pony's mouth. This is called contact.

If the pony is well trained, it will respond to your aids.

Squeeze the pony's sides with your legs to show that you want to go forward. If the pony is lazy, nudge with your heels. Kick only when you have to.

If your pony has a very sensitive mouth, you need only light contact.

Learning how to turn

You need to learn how to turn so that you can steer your pony. As you begin to understand each other, you will be able to make better turns and circles. Apart from using your aids, remember to look where you are trying to go. It is surprising how much this will help you. Here, you can find out how to turn left. To turn right, simply give your pony the opposite aids.

The pony's neck begins to bend to the left as you give the aids.

Using your hands

Feel the left rein gently, until the pony turns its head left. As it begins to turn, let your right hand move forward, like this. Keep the contact with the pony's mouth.

Using your inside leg

Press inward with your left leg, which is your inside leg, to encourage the pony to keep going forward. Try to imagine that you are turning the pony around this leg.

If you are using your aids properly, the pony's whole body will bend in the direction that it is turning.

Turn your head to look where you are going as your pony starts to turn left.

Using your outside leg

Place your right leg, which is your outside leg, just behind the girth. This stops the pony from swinging out its hindquarters as you turn left.

Halt to walk

Sit up straight, and push with your seat by tucking your bottom under. Close your legs on the pony's sides. As the pony responds to your aids, let your hands move forward. Now the pony will understand that it can walk on.

Tuck your bottom under.

Press the pony's sides equally with both legs.

Walking on

Now stop using your leg aids. Let your lower half move with the pony, and keep your top half still. Allow your hands to move forward and backward with the pony's head.

Keep your top half still.

Stop using your legs, unless your pony is lazy.

Walk to halt

To slow down to a halt, straighten your back and keep your hands still. Try not to let the pony move its head forward. You may need to pull a little on the reins, but as soon as your pony responds, stop pulling the reins.

Straighten your back.

Keep your legs against the pony's sides.

Learning to trot

THE FIRST TIME that you trot will probably feel very bumpy and jerky. But it becomes much less bumpy as you learn to rise up and down in the saddle. The posting or rising trot is quite easy to do. On one stride you sit in the saddle, on the next you let the pony bounce you slightly out of the saddle. After a while, you will be able to go up and down in time to the movement of the pony. The posting trot is the most comfortable pace when you are riding out, especially when the pony is trotting quickly. Learning the sitting trot is important, too. The sitting trot is used for many of the school movements that you will learn about later. You also need to know how to do the sitting trot properly before you can learn to canter.

The posting trot
Try going up and down in the saddle while your pony is standing still. It is even easier once you are trotting.

Look up, and concentrate on keeping your balance.

As you go up, push down in the stirrups with your heels.

These yellow bandages help you to see how a pony's legs trot in diagonal pairs.

How a pony trots
In a trot, the pony moves its legs in "diagonal pairs." One front hoof and the back hoof on the opposite side are on the ground at the same time, followed by the other two hooves at the same time. This pony has bandages on two legs so that you can see the diagonal pairs very clearly.

Good balance
If it is difficult to balance in a posting trot because your pony is lazy and you have to keep kicking, your instructor may give you a crop, to encourage the pony to go forward.

Walk to trot
To make the transition from walk to trot, shorten your reins very slightly so that they are not slack when the pony goes into a trot. This will help you keep control. Sit up tall and squeeze firmly with your legs or nudge the pony's sides with your feet to ask it to trot on.

Sit up tall and straight.

Do not pull back on the pony's mouth.

If your pony is lazy, one or two hard kicks is better than flapping your legs.

By holding on to the pommel at first, you can pull yourself more deeply into the saddle.

Your pony's back will move up and down as it trots. You will learn to balance as you become used to this.

The lunge line is attached to a type of halter, called a cavesson, on the pony's head.

The instructor is able to control your pony with the lunge line and a crop, so that you can concentrate on your riding position.

Trotting
on a lunge line
Once you are a confident rider, you can have lessons on a lunge line to improve. This will teach you how to do a sitting trot without losing your balance and tugging on the pony's mouth. During these lessons, your instructor may ask you to trot with your feet out of the stirrups. This exercise helps you to develop a deeper seat.

By trotting with your feet out of the stirrups, you will learn to absorb the movement of the trot without bouncing out of the saddle.

Trotting
As the pony breaks into a trot, try to stay in the saddle for a few paces, until you have settled into a rhythm. The pony's head and neck will seem to stay more still now. Try to keep your hands still, too.

Keep your hands still.

Keep an even contact with the pony's mouth.

Do not go into a posting trot until you have settled into a rhythm.

Trot to walk
If you want to slow down to a walk, sit up tall, keep your legs still, and gently pull on the reins. As soon as the pony goes into walk, let your hands move forward and backward with the pony's head and neck.

Try to push your weight down in your heels, even when you have to kick.

You should not need to use your legs very much to keep your pony going at the same pace.

Exercises in the saddle

FEELING CONFIDENT on your pony is one of the most important parts of riding. Having confidence affects the way that you ride, and the way that your pony behaves. There are many exercises that you can do with your pony to make you more confident and relaxed in the saddle. With practice, you will soon be as comfortable on a pony as you are on the ground. These exercises are fun to do, and help you have more control over your pony. The more you learn to trust the pony, the more it will trust you, and the better you will ride.

How to go "around-the-world"

1 First, take both feet out of the stirrups. Hold on to the front of the saddle with your right hand, and the back with your left hand. Swing your right leg over the pommel (at the front of the saddle) so that you are sitting sidesaddle. Adjust your hands as you move around, so that you always have one hand on the saddle.

Try not to lean back too far, in case you lose your balance.

🐎 **Ask an adult to help**
When you do these exercises, there must always be an adult holding your pony. Never try these exercises on your own.

Make sure that you do not kick the pony as you swing your legs.

2 Swing your left leg over the cantle (at the back), followed by your right leg. Then swing your left leg over the pommel so that you are facing forward. Now you have been "around-the-world."

An outdoor lesson
Once you are more confident, you will enjoy group lessons. These children are doing exercises outdoors while their ponies are walking along. This is safe as long as an instructor is present, and if you keep hold of the reins.

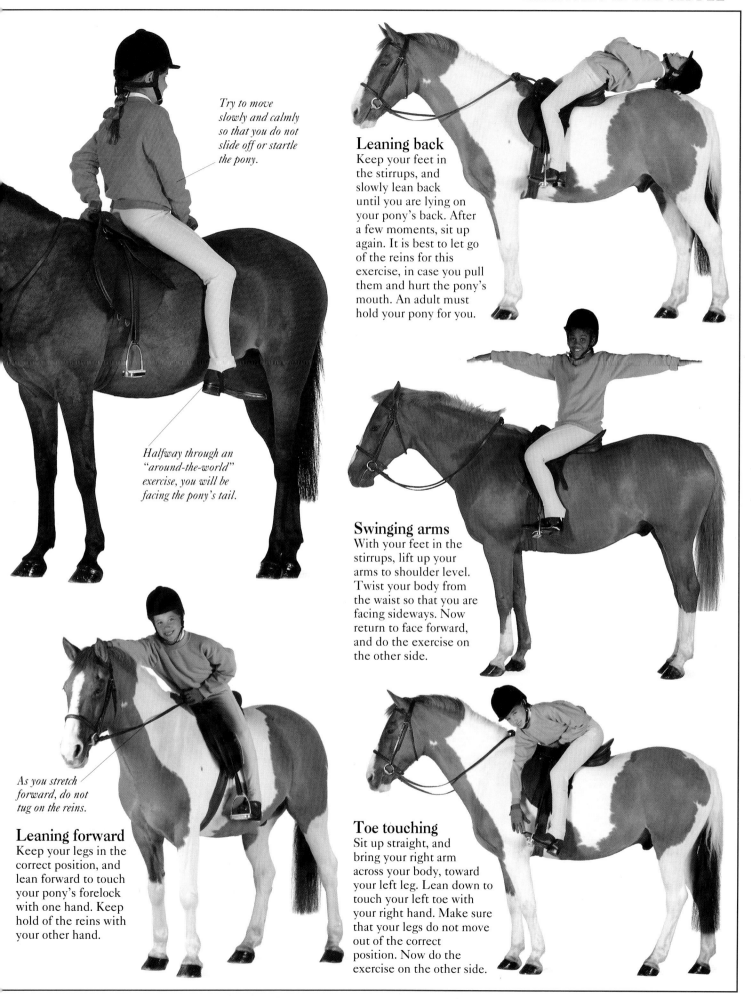

Try to move slowly and calmly so that you do not slide off or startle the pony.

Halfway through an "around-the-world" exercise, you will be facing the pony's tail.

Leaning back
Keep your feet in the stirrups, and slowly lean back until you are lying on your pony's back. After a few moments, sit up again. It is best to let go of the reins for this exercise, in case you pull them and hurt the pony's mouth. An adult must hold your pony for you.

Swinging arms
With your feet in the stirrups, lift up your arms to shoulder level. Twist your body from the waist so that you are facing sideways. Now return to face forward, and do the exercise on the other side.

As you stretch forward, do not tug on the reins.

Leaning forward
Keep your legs in the correct position, and lean forward to touch your pony's forelock with one hand. Keep hold of the reins with your other hand.

Toe touching
Sit up straight, and bring your right arm across your body, toward your left leg. Lean down to touch your left toe with your right hand. Make sure that your legs do not move out of the correct position. Now do the exercise on the other side.

21

Cantering and galloping

ONCE YOU CAN trot confidently, you are ready to canter, which is faster and more exciting. You will probably learn how to canter in an arena, where the ground is smooth. Your instructor may put a neck strap on the pony at first, so that you can hold it for extra security if you feel unsafe. Holding on to the neck strap to help you balance is much kinder than holding on by pulling on the pony's mouth. You may find that your pony takes a little bit of persuasion to move into canter, but most ponies enjoy cantering. When you feel confident, you will probably want to go even faster. So ease off the reins a little, and use your legs to urge your pony to canter more quickly. Soon you may find that you are galloping. This is great fun, too, as long as you learn to keep your balance at the canter first.

Running free

Ponies love to canter around and play when they are turned out in the field. So it is important that the field is safely fenced, with no sharp objects lying on the ground.

Leading off

Go into a sitting trot for a few paces before you give the aids to canter. Sit up, and keep the contact with your pony's mouth. With your inside leg on the girth and your outside leg slightly behind it, squeeze the pony's sides. It will feel like a little hop as your pony "leads off" into a canter.

Preparing to canter

Make sure that you are in a good, balanced trot before you ask your pony to canter. It is best to ask for a canter when you are moving in a circle or curve, so that the pony will understand that it should lead off (start to canter) on the leg that is on the inside of the curve.

If you feel nervous when you first canter, you could ask another person to lead your pony on a lunge line.

A sitting trot is best if you want to go into canter.

As your pony "leads off", try to sit up straight.

Keep the contact with the pony's mouth.

The pony should be in a trot before you ask for the canter.

Squeeze with both legs to encourage your pony to canter.

Even foals like to join in with the others.

Galloping

Once you can canter properly, you will learn how to have a "forward seat" for galloping. The forward seat gives the horse the freedom to go faster. First, shorten your stirrups so that it is easier to balance, and keep your weight down in your heels. Then shorten your reins and lean forward so that your seat is slightly out of the saddle. In this way you will absorb the movement of the horse through your knees and heels rather than through your seat.

You can see how the back legs are pushing this horse forward as it gallops, so it covers more ground than in a canter.

The canter

As your pony starts to canter, try to keep your bottom in the saddle. This is difficult at first, but it becomes easier if you relax a little. Your back should stay straight, and your hips should move with the rocking movement of the canter. Let your hands follow the movement of the pony's head and neck. If you do not, the pony may think that you want to go back into a trot.

Canter to trot

Make sure that your canter is steady and balanced before you ask the pony to move into a trot. When you want to slow down, stop squeezing with your legs, keep your hips still, sit back, and take a firmer hold on the reins until your pony moves back into a trot.

 Confident cantering
Wait until you are confident at the trot before you attempt to canter.

 **Road sense**
Cantering or galloping on a road can be dangerous, as it is easy for the pony to slip.

Keep your back straight, try not to slouch, and keep your bottom in the saddle.

Let your hands go with the movement of the pony's head and neck.

Allow your hips to move with the flow of the canter.

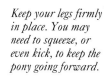

Keep your legs firmly in place. You may need to squeeze, or even kick, to keep the pony going forward.

Riding with others

ONCE YOU ARE able to control your pony, you can begin to concentrate on your style and skill as a rider. Now your instructor will teach you to ride with others in a group lesson. You will learn how to pass other ponies in an arena, and how to keep your distance from the pony in front. Your instructor will also teach you how to do special riding exercises called "school movements." These include riding in circles, half circles, and figure eights. To improve your style, sit up as still and straight as you can in the saddle, and try to make your aids as unnoticeable as possible. But do not make them so unnoticeable that your pony cannot understand your signals.

The rider at the front is "leading file." She has to set the pace, or speed, of all the riders.

There should be at least the length of a pony between each of the riders.

Keeping your distance
Your pony will probably be more interested and easier to keep going, when you are riding with others. But you may find that your pony always tries to catch up with the pony in front. If this happens, give the slowing down aids in plenty of time, and use your voice to steady your pony.

Passing each other
If your instructor asks you to warm up your pony, you can ride around the arena wherever you like. But you must be aware of others, especially if you are going in opposite directions. Depending on where you are riding, there will be rules to remember about how to pass other ponies so that you do not bump into each other. Always pay attention to your instructor.

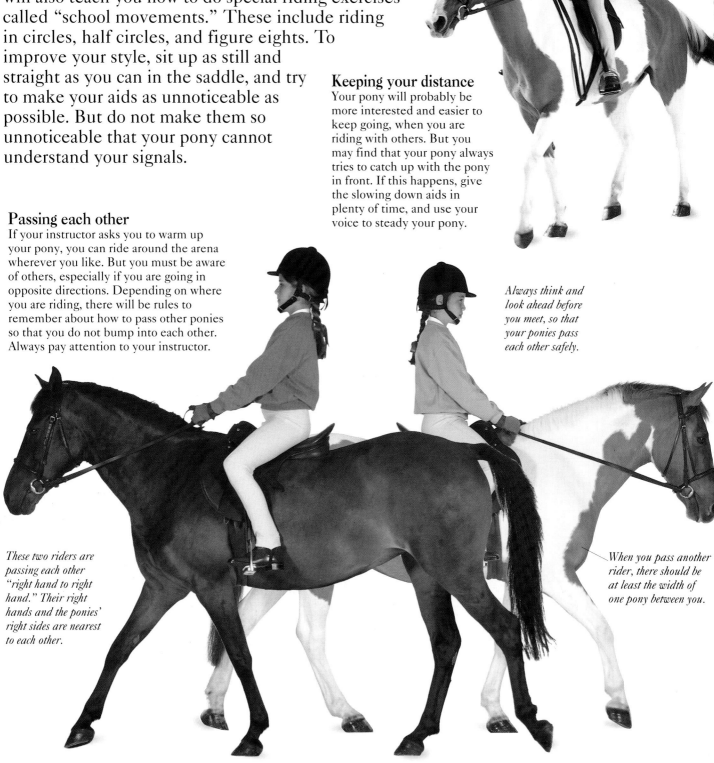

Always think and look ahead before you meet, so that your ponies pass each other safely.

These two riders are passing each other "right hand to right hand." Their right hands and the ponies' right sides are nearest to each other.

When you pass another rider, there should be at least the width of one pony between you.

With so much to think about, make sure that you do not bump into the pony in front, or your pony may be kicked.

An instructor usually puts the slowest pony at the back so that it does not slow the others down.

The dressage arena

A dressage arena has markers with letters on them around the sides. The markers are for school movements, so you should learn where they all are. There are also three imaginary letters, "G," "X," and "D," down the center that you need to learn.

An arena is 130 to 190ft (40 to 60m) long.

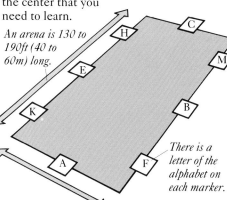

There is a letter of the alphabet on each marker.

School movements

Once you know where the markers are in the arena, you can learn how to do exercises called "school movements." These exercises include riding in a circle, making a turn, and "changing reins" (changing your direction). Your instructor will ask you to do a school movement at a particular marker in the arena.

Making circles

During your lesson, you may be asked to ride your pony around part of the arena in a large or a small circle.

Figure eights

You may learn how to ride around the arena in a figure eight, which is a way to practice changing reins.

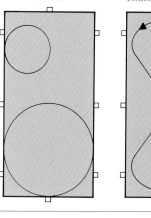

Practicing in a group

When you can do school movements properly on your pony, it is fun to practice with others in a group. These three young riders are turning across the arena at the same time, instead of in single file. When you are turning like this, you need to concentrate hard.

As the pony begins to turn left, let your right hand move forward a little.

Adjust your speed so that you stay in line with the leading file.

Turn your head as your pony turns, and keep an eye on the rider in front.

Press inward with your inside leg to encourage the pony to turn.

Learning to jump

Keep your head up and look ahead.

Keep your back straight. It may help if you stick your bottom out.

J UMPING WELL depends on good balance, and you may only feel safe after you have jumped many times. Your introduction to jumping may be ground poles laid on the ground. These poles help you become used to the way that the pony's stride changes as it goes over an obstacle. Once you can keep your balance over the poles, your instructor may put a small jump at the end of the line of poles. He or she may lead you over the jumps until you are confident enough to jump on your own. Do not worry if you fall off your pony - it is easy to lose your balance at first. There is a saying that you are not a true rider until you have fallen off at least seven times!

Once you have found your balance, you will be able to move your hands freely.

The correct jumping position

It is important to learn the correct jumping position because this is the best way to keep your balance and give your pony a chance to jump correctly. Try to keep your head up as you jump. This helps your style as well as allowing you to see where you are going. Concentrate on keeping your back straight, and let your weight sink into your heels.

Allow your weight to sink down into your heels, and keep the ball of your foot on the stirrup.

Shortening your stirrups

Always shorten your stirrups evenly before you jump to help you keep your balance. With your foot in the stirrup, pull the buckle out with one hand. Pull the buckle up the leather a few holes. If you keep your first finger on the pin it is easier to push the pin into the correct hole.

To stop yourself from bouncing up and down as your pony trots over the poles, try to absorb the movement in your back, knees, and ankles.

Riding over ground poles

Ground poles can help both the rider and the pony to improve their jumping. It also gives you a chance to practice your jumping position and find your balance. It may feel bumpy when you first ride over the poles, but try to relax, and absorb the pony's movement through your knees, ankles, and back.

Never pull on the pony's mouth. If you begin to lose your balance, ask for a neck strap to hold on to.

Your instructor will make sure that these ground poles are the correct distance apart from each other.

How a pony learns to jump

Ponies have a natural ability to jump, but some enjoy it more than others, so they are trained over small fences at first. A pony can learn to jump with someone on its back, but most ponies find it easier without a rider. This pony in this picture is being taught to jump on a lunge line.

If you feel nervous, hold the neck strap. This helps you to stay on, and stops you from tugging on the pony's mouth.

Jumping on a lead line

If you are eager to try jumping but are not completely in control of your pony, ask an experienced adult to run alongside you, leading your pony over a small fence. This is one way to become used to the feel of a jump without worrying about your steering or your speed.

The other end of this lead line must be long enough to allow the pony freedom to move its head and neck as it jumps over the fence.

Keep moving

Always move your pony forward toward a fence, and use your legs to encourage it.

Prepare yourself

Make sure that you feel ready before you jump a fence. You cannot expect your pony to jump if you do not want to.

Ground poles leading to a jump

For this, you need to concentrate on going forward, keeping your balance, and staying in the correct jumping position. Always wait for your pony to take off before you lean forward yourself. Ground poles leading up to a jump help the pony take off over the jump in the correct place.

Allow your hands to follow the movement of the pony's head and neck as it jumps.

Make sure that there is plenty of space between you and the pony in front, in case the leader knocks down the jump.

Keep looking up and ahead, even when you arrive in front of the fence.

The stages of a jump

FOR MOST RIDERS, jumping is the biggest thrill of all. Your main task when you are jumping is to keep your pony going forward, in a balanced way, to meet the fences. If you do this properly, your pony will be able to decide where to take off and how to jump. One of the secrets of jumping is to sit still as you are approaching a fence, but be ready to kick if your pony slows down. It is always best to learn to jump on an experienced pony, until you have found your balance. One day, you may find yourself jumping over big fences on a beautiful horse, like the one that I am riding here.

Look up and ahead, between the horse's ears. This helps you to keep your back straight, as well as helping you see where you are going.

Once you have taken off, give a little more rein with your hands. Nothing puts a horse off jumping more than being pulled on the mouth by the rider.

The horse lifts its forelegs up high as it takes off, over the jump.

As a horse takes off, the hindquarters will come right underneath the body to enable the horse to spring up.

This type of jump can be knocked down if the horse hits it. But cross-country fences are solid, so if the horse hits them hard, both horse and rider could fall.

The horse pushes off with both back feet.

The takeoff

The horse takes off a few feet in front of the fence, about the same distance away as the height of the fence. It is up to the horse to decide where to take off, so just keep going forward. Your horse may want to move in a little closer before jumping, to have a look at the obstacle first. Just try to keep your balance and sit still as the horse takes off. You will find that your body automatically swings forward with the horse. Remember to allow your horse's head as much freedom as it needs to stretch for the fence.

In midair

As the horse jumps over the fence, keep your lower legs underneath you, with your weight down through your heels. Allow as much rein as the horse needs by letting your arms stretch forward with the movement of the head and neck as they stretch over the fence.

The horse must have the freedom to stretch its neck out in order to jump in good style and to stretch over a big fence.

Jumping can be bumpy
Do not be surprised if you find that jumping is uncomfortable at first. With plenty of practice, it will feel more comfortable.

Say "thank you"
When you have jumped a fence successfully, remember to thank your horse or pony with a pat.

On landing, give the horse as much extra rein as it needs by letting your arms stretch forward.

When you are in midair, keep the lower part of your legs straight underneath your body.

A horse always lands with one foreleg leading, so for an instant all the weight of horse and rider is taken by just one of the horse's legs.

Landing

On landing, you must continue to allow the horse freedom of its head. Landing may feel bumpy, so keep your lower legs under you, or swing them a little further forward, with your heels down, to absorb the shock of landing. Try not to let your legs swing back or lean on the horse's neck with your hands. As soon as the horse has landed, you can take up more contact with the bit once again, and make any adjustments to your pace or direction before the next fence.

Advanced jumping

I F YOU ENJOY jumping, and feel confident, you could try some cross-country fences. The biggest fences are often the easiest to jump, as long as you approach them boldly. The most difficult fences are those where your pony cannot see what is on the other side until just before it takes off. It takes years of training for any horse or pony to jump fences like these, and they must have great trust in their riders. The horses that I ride can usually sense how much I enjoy the challenge of cross-country fences, and they respond well.

This rider is just about to push her lower legs further forward, to brace herself for landing.

Banks
This Normandy bank has a fence at the far side, so the rider has to jump over the fence and off the bank in one leap.

A pony can be afraid to jump sometimes, just as a rider can be afraid.

Refusals and run outs
If your pony stops in front of a fence, this is called a "refusal." Running to the side of a fence is a "run out." Your instructor can help you solve these problems.

The horse's pricked ears show that it is happy, and has confidence in the rider.

Hedges
Most ponies and horses enjoy jumping hedges. But hedges can be quite big, so you should always approach them in a positive, confident way so your pony takes off with a big, bold leap.

Look before you leap
If you want to jump a hedge when you are out on a ride, check first to make sure that it is safe to jump.

Check for thorns
After you have been jumping over hedges, check your pony's legs for any scratches or thorns.

In this picture, I am just about to turn my horse right on landing.

Water jumps

In cross-country competitions, you often have to jump into water or ride through it. If the water is deep, it is difficult for the horse to move quickly. Never hurry, but make sure that you keep encouraging the horse to move forward.

In this picture, both horse and rider are in excellent balance.

Steps

Steps are like a staircase. Sometimes there is a jump at the top or bottom, so it is important to be in good balance. Keep the horse full of energy without rushing.

Bounce fence

A bounce fence, or in-and-out, is when two fences are so close together that there is no room for the horse to take a stride between them. The horse lands after the first fence, then takes off immediately, over the second fence.

The instructor must place the fences the correct distance apart, or it could confuse the horse and be dangerous.

When you are practicing, it is best to use low jumps, especially at first.

Trail riding

SOON YOU WILL discover the excitement of riding through the countryside with a group of friends. Trail riding, or hacking, is great fun and is something to look forward to when you are a confident and capable rider. You will be able to canter across fields, trot through forests and woods, and ride through shallow streams. Riding on uneven ground helps to improve your balance and your pony's. At the end of a ride, your pony may be hot, so walk the last part, on a long rein, with a loosened girth. If your pony's coat is muddy, wash it down when you arrive back at the stable, then rub it down with a towel.

Pony trekking

In many parts of the world, people of all ages enjoy long rides, called treks, in the mountains, across the countryside, or by the sea. There are several kinds of treks, either for half a day or a whole day. People also enjoy pony trekking holidays, which is a lovely way to explore new places with your pony. If you go pony trekking, make sure that you wear your riding hat and gloves, even if other riders are not wearing them.

Ask permission
If you want to leave a bridle trail and ride across the fields, ask the owner's permission first.

Shut the gate
Whenever you open a gate, always close it behind you.

Check the ground
Look out for sharp stones that could hurt your pony's hooves.

Riding through woods
When you are riding in the woods, stay on the trails and look out for low branches. Your pony will look out for itself, but you may have to duck sometimes. Go slowly along tracks where there are tree roots and logs to trip your pony. Your pony is unlikely to fall, but if it stumbles, you could fall off.

Riding in open country
Most ponies enjoy a ride, especially with others. You may find that your pony becomes excited and pulls, which can be uncomfortable. If this happens, calm your pony and ask others not to ride too close.

An experienced adult will go with you when you first start trail riding.

Your clothes can be as formal or as casual as you like. But try to look neat.

Keep your distance from each other, just in case one pony kicks in excitement.

How to open and close a gate

1 Some gates can be opened only if you dismount from your pony first. But it is useful to learn how to open and close a gate without dismounting. While you are mounted, position your pony so that you can lean down to reach the latch on the gate. As you do this, make sure that the reins do not get caught. With both reins in one hand, undo the latch with the other, and push the gate open.

Riding through water

Ponies do not usually mind water, but never ride through deep water unless an experienced adult is with you. If your pony is not used to water, you may need to give it plenty of encouragement.

2 If possible, hold the gate as the pony walks forward. When the gate is open wide enough, use your aids to ask the pony to move its hindquarters around in a half circle, while it keeps its forelegs still enough for you to hold the gate open.

3 Once you are on the other side of the gate, ask your pony to walk forward so that you can close the gate. If you let go of the gate, be careful that it does not swing back and hit the pony. Fasten the gate properly before you ride off.

Soak the sweaty and muddy areas with a sponge.

Washing down after a ride

Wet the muddy areas with a hose or a bucket of water and sponge. Then use a sweat scraper to remove the excess water from the pony's coat. Scrape downward, and be gentle on bony and sensitive areas.

Riding on the road

BEFORE YOU ARE ready to ride on a road, you should be an experienced rider and know the traffic laws. You must also be able to control your pony in traffic. Riding on roads can be dangerous, so a rider needs to be alert at all times. The first few times that you ride on the road, your instructor will probably take you in a group. You will either ride in pairs or in single file, with the most experienced riders at the front and at the back of the group. Good manners and common sense are very important when you are road riding. Try to be polite to other road users, and be aware of what is happening around you. Learn how to give the correct hand signals, and look, listen, and think ahead at all times.

Good manners

It is important to thank drivers who stop for you or slow down to let you pass. The easiest way to thank others is simply to put up your hand, smile, and say "Thank you."

You can warn others to slow down by holding your arm out like this, and slowly waving it up and down.

Shy pony

If your pony is nervous, and shies when you pass a vehicle, ride forward as calmly as you can, and use your leg to stop the pony from swinging its hindquarters out into the road. Never ride too close to any vehicle, in case the driver starts the engine or opens a door.

Hand signals

When you give a hand signal, it must be very clear so that other people can see exactly what you mean. When you think that it is safe to turn, give your signal as clearly as possible, and wait for the driver to see your signal. As you begin to turn left or right, keep checking in front and behind.

Look all around before you signal, and make sure that the driver has noticed you.

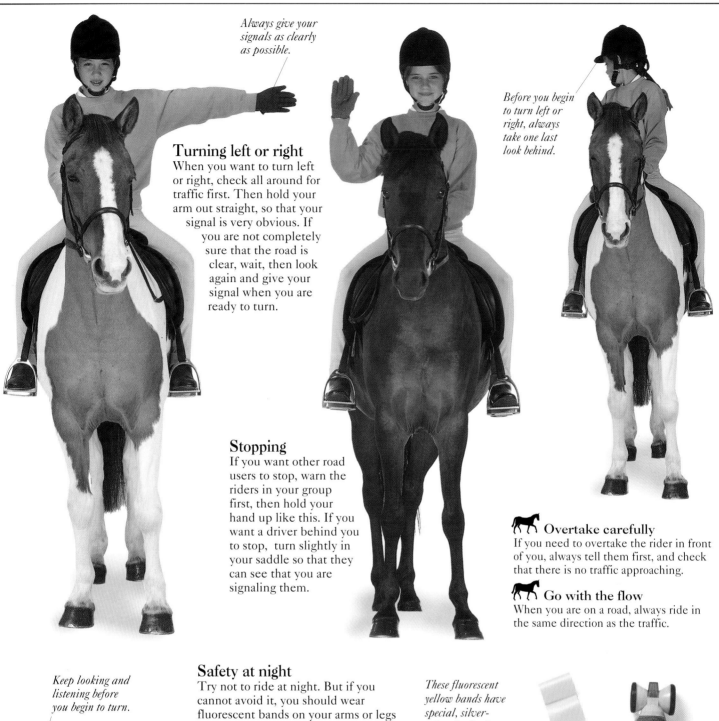

Always give your signals as clearly as possible.

Before you begin to turn left or right, always take one last look behind.

Turning left or right

When you want to turn left or right, check all around for traffic first. Then hold your arm out straight, so that your signal is very obvious. If you are not completely sure that the road is clear, wait, then look again and give your signal when you are ready to turn.

Stopping

If you want other road users to stop, warn the riders in your group first, then hold your hand up like this. If you want a driver behind you to stop, turn slightly in your saddle so that they can see that you are signaling them.

Overtake carefully

If you need to overtake the rider in front of you, always tell them first, and check that there is no traffic approaching.

Go with the flow

When you are on a road, always ride in the same direction as the traffic.

Safety at night

Try not to ride at night. But if you cannot avoid it, you should wear fluorescent bands on your arms or legs that have special, silver-colored strips on them. The silver strips glow brightly if a car headlight shines on them. You can also put these bands on your pony's legs for extra safety.

Keep looking and listening before you begin to turn.

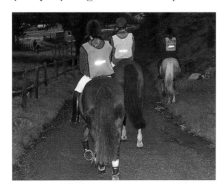

These fluorescent yellow bands have special, silver-colored reflective strips on them.

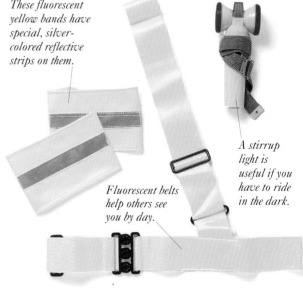

A stirrup light is useful if you have to ride in the dark.

Fluorescent belts help others see you by day.

What a pony wears

EVERY RIDER NEEDS to learn what each piece of tack is called, and why it is used. Using the correct equipment makes learning to ride safer and easier for both the rider and pony. Tack consists mainly of the saddle and bridle, which are usually made of leather. A saddle is used for several reasons. It makes riding more comfortable for you and the pony, and it has stirrups attached to it, which help keep you in the saddle. A bridle is used because it gives you contact with the bit in the pony's mouth, so that you have some control over the pony. There are many other pieces of equipment that you can use for riding, but it takes an experienced person to know what kind of tack suits your pony best.

The headstall fits behind the ears and down each side of the pony's head.

The browband lies across the forehead. It stops the headstall from sliding back.

The throatlatch passes under the jaw when you fasten the bridle.

The cheekpieces buckle on to both sides of the headstall and hold the bit in the pony's mouth.

The noseband lies around the pony's nose. This cavesson noseband is the simplest noseband.

This is a jointed eggbutt snaffle bit. It is buckled on to the cheek pieces.

The reins are attached to either side of the bit. They are buckled together at the other end and they are placed over the pony's head, ready for the rider to pick up.

Bridles
The bridle fits on the head and holds the bit in place. There are several types of bridle, including double bridles, which are for advanced training. This pony is wearing a snaffle bridle.

Bits
There are many types of bits, such as snaffles and pelhams. Bits can be made of metal, rubber, or other materials. All have rings or cheekpieces on either side of the mouthpiece to stop them sliding through the mouth.

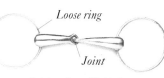

Loose ring

Joint

A jointed snaffle bit has a joint in the middle.

Eggbutt joint

This is an eggbutt snaffle bit with a straight bar.

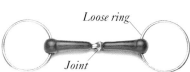

Loose ring

Joint

This is a loose, ring, jointed snaffle bit, made of rubber.

The lead rope clips onto a ring on the halter.

The halter
This piece of tack gives you control over the pony when you are not riding. It is made up of a headstall, a noseband, and a throatlatch, with buckles on each piece so that you can adjust it to fit. A halter makes it easier to catch, lead, and tie up your pony.

A handsome leather halter is often used for shows.

This halter is made of nylon.

Girths
This is attached to either side of the saddle, and passes under the pony's belly, behind the "elbows" to keep the saddle in place. Girths can be made of leather, and also string, cotton, or synthetic materials.

These overreach boots fit around the front pasterns to protect the heels from being cut by the back hooves.

Boots
Ponies sometimes need to wear boots to protect their legs during exercise. There are several kinds, including these brushing boots and overreach boots.

Brushing boots are usually padded on the inside.

This type of girth is called a leather "balding."

Saddles

A saddle is designed to be comfortable both for horse and rider, and it is particularly important that it fits correctly. It has padded panels underneath, to keep the pressure off the pony's spine. All horses' and ponies' backs are shaped differently, so an experienced person must fit the saddle. If you stand behind the pony when the saddle is on (without a saddle pad) you should be able to see daylight all the way along the spine.

The pommel is the front part of the saddle. It is shaped so that it does not press down on the pony's spine.

The seat is the deepest part of the saddle, where you should sit.

The cantle is the highest part at the back of the saddle.

The saddle pad absorbs sweat and grease. It fits between the pony's back and the saddle.

Saddle flap

Some saddles have a padded area on the saddle flap, which can make them more comfortable for the rider.

This flap, called the buckle guard, covers the buckles and protects the saddle flap.

The buckles on the girth must be checked regularly to make sure that they are secure.

This saddle pad has a loop for the girth to pass through. It helps to prevent the pad from slipping out from under the saddle.

Most saddles have a loop to put the spare end of the stirrup leather through.

Stirrups

These are attached to the saddle by stirrup leathers. Stirrups must be the correct width so that your feet cannot become stuck in them. Most stirrups are made of stainless steel, and you can fit rubber treads into the bottom of them to give your feet extra grip.

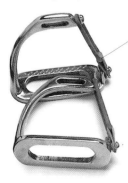

These safety stirrups are sometimes used for children. If you fall off, the band on the side comes undone, so your foot can come out of the stirrup.

This wide, padded strap is called a roller, and it keeps the blanket in place. A roller often has a breastband around the pony's chest to keep it in place.

Blankets

There are many types of blankets. Some are for wearing in the stable, and others are for wearing outdoors. Some ponies are given a waterproof New Zealand blanket to wear when they are turned out, to protect them from the wind and rain.

On a cold day, a wool blanket like this one helps to keep a pony warm.

This fillet string stops the back of the blanket from flapping up over the pony's back if the wind blows it.

Tacking up – the saddle

A WELL-TRAINED PONY does not usually mind being tacked up, and should stand still for you while you put on its saddle and bridle. But ponies are often quick to learn bad habits, and some like to move around while you are tacking up. This means that you could end up chasing your pony with the saddle. So the first few times you put a pony's tack on, someone will help you do it properly. It is best to put a halter on the pony and tie it up before you begin. Ponies should have their own saddle and bridle, which fit them properly. When you put the saddle on, make sure that it sits comfortably on the pony, not too far back or too far forward. A saddle needs to be checked for damage every so often to make sure that it is safe. You can check it yourself by looking for loose stitching or leather that is tearing. If you discover something, ask an experienced adult to have a look, too.

Carry the saddle with the pommel toward your elbow, like this.

Carrying the tack

When you collect your pony's tack from the tack room, hang the bridle over your left shoulder. Place the saddle on your left arm, with the pommel toward your elbow. Make sure that the girth is laid over the top of the saddle before you leave the tack room, and check that there are no dangling straps that could trip you up.

Check that none of these straps are trailing behind you when you are carrying your pony's tack.

How to put on a saddle

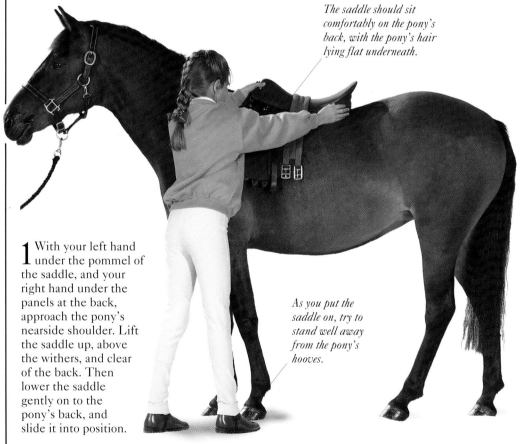

The saddle should sit comfortably on the pony's back, with the pony's hair lying flat underneath.

As you put the saddle on, try to stand well away from the pony's hooves.

1 With your left hand under the pommel of the saddle, and your right hand under the panels at the back, approach the pony's nearside shoulder. Lift the saddle up, above the withers, and clear of the back. Then lower the saddle gently on to the pony's back, and slide it into position.

2 Walk around the front of the pony to the other side and let down the girth so that the loose end dangles down. Make sure that it is not twisted. Then walk back around the front to the pony's nearside. Reach under the pony for the girth, and buckle it up.

How to take off a saddle

1 First, run up each of the stirrup irons. To do this, hold the stirrup leather away from the saddle, and slide the stirrup up the strap beneath, as far as the buckle.

2 Hold the stirrup in place at the top of the leather, and tuck the leather through the stirrup iron. The leather should lie flat against the saddle, with the stirrup at the top.

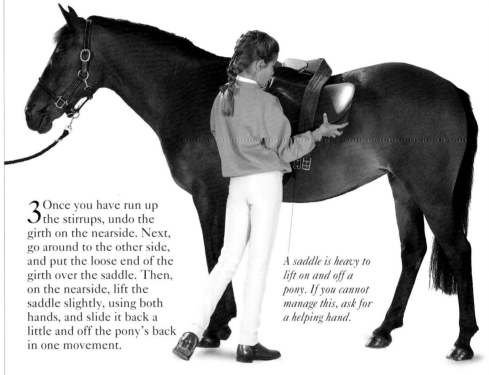

If you carry the pony's tack in the correct way, you will always have one hand free to open a door if you need to.

3 Once you have run up the stirrups, undo the girth on the nearside. Next, go around to the other side, and put the loose end of the girth over the saddle. Then, on the nearside, lift the saddle slightly, using both hands, and slide it back a little and off the pony's back in one movement.

A saddle is heavy to lift on and off a pony. If you cannot manage this, ask for a helping hand.

4 Pull down the buckle guard so that it covers the buckles. This will stop them from pressing into the saddle flap and damaging it. Finally, check that the girth is comfortable for the pony, and that no loose skin is caught underneath.

3 Lift up the saddle flap, then fasten the buckle on the left girth strap, and all the other buckles to the same notch. Check that the girth is tight enough. You should just be able to slide three fingers underneath it.

Setting down the saddle
A saddle is valuable. If you have to put it on the ground, lower it gently, and lean the cantle against a wall, well away from your pony's hooves. Never leave the saddle on a stable door or leaning against it. The best place to put a saddle is on a wooden or metal saddle horse.

Safe saddle
Take care never to leave the girth undone when you are putting on the saddle. If the pony started to move off, the saddle could slip off its back and be damaged.

Breathe in
Some ponies breathe in when you are doing up their girth so that it is loose. If your pony does this, you can tighten the girth after leading the pony around.

Tacking up – the bridle

I T TAKES PRACTICE to learn how to put a bridle on properly, and you may find that your pony likes to play a game when you try to do this. If the pony keeps lifting its head up too high for you to reach, ask a taller person to help you. Most ponies do not mind having a bridle put on, and they soon learn not to mind having the bit in their mouths, because it does not hurt them. But when you are placing the bit, remember not to put your fingers inside the pony's mouth, just in case you are bitten by mistake. Each pony's bridle should fit well and also be comfortable to wear, so it is very important that you learn how to put one on properly.

The bit

The bit must fit the pony's mouth so that it is comfortable. It lies over the tongue and across the bars of the mouth. The bars are the areas of the mouth where there are no teeth.

Too wide

This bit is too wide for the pony's jaw. It could slide across the mouth and be uncomfortable.

Placing the bit

If this is difficult to do, slip your thumb into the corner of the pony's mouth. This will make the pony open its mouth.

Too low

This bit is too low in the pony's mouth. It could bang against the teeth and be uncomfortable.

A perfect fit

This bit is comfortable. You can tell by the wrinkles, called smiles, at the corner of the mouth.

 Neat reins are best

Never leave the reins hanging in loops. Your pony's legs could become tangled up in them.

Leather tastes good

Some ponies chew any leather that they find. So keep the noseband and reins out of reach.

How to put on a bridle

1 Check that the throatlatch and noseband are undone. Then stand on the pony's nearside and place the reins over its head. Slip your right hand under the jaw and up, onto the pony's nose, to give you control. With the bridle in your right hand, guide the bit into the mouth with your other hand.

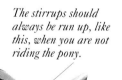

The stirrups should always be run up, like this, when you are not riding the pony.

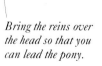

Bring the reins over the head so that you can lead the pony.

All tacked up

Once you are used to tacking up, you will be able to see at a glance if the saddle is in the right position, and if the bit and noseband are adjusted correctly. Now your pony is ready to go for a ride.

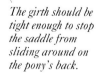

The girth should be tight enough to stop the saddle from sliding around on the pony's back.

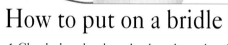

Bend the ears under the headstall, rather than trying to lift the bridle over them, or you will pull the pony's mouth.

Buckle up the noseband after you have done up the throatlatch.

2 Lift the headstall over the ears and take the forelock out from under the browband. Loosely buckle the throatlatch and check that you can fit four fingers between the jawbone and throatlatch. Adjust the buckle if you need to. Check that the bit is at the right height in the pony's mouth, adjusting the cheekpieces if necessary.

Checking the noseband
You should be able to place two of your fingers just underneath the noseband.

3 Place the noseband across the front of the nose, and slip it under the cheekbones to buckle it. The noseband should lie straight across the nose, the width of two fingers below the cheekbone. If it is not straight, check the buckle on the cheekpiece.

How to take off a bridle
You can stand in front or beside your pony to take off the bridle. First, unfasten the noseband and the throatlatch. Bring the reins up the neck to just behind the ears. Then stand next to, or in front of, the pony. Take the headstall and reins in both hands, and lift off the bridle.

If your pony is quiet, you can take the bridle off in this way. Stand far enough back, in case the pony lifts its head up.

If your pony moves around, it may be best to take off the bridle like this.

Looking after the tack

Oiling the tack
Leather tack should be oiled sometimes to keep it in good condition. But never oil the top of your saddle because it will be slippery to sit on, and it will rub off on your jodhpurs and stain them.

A PONY'S TACK needs to be well looked after, just like a pony itself. Leather tack is expensive, and if it is not well cared for, it can dry up and crack. This makes it uncomfortable for the pony and dangerous for the rider. So a saddle and bridle must be cleaned first with water and then with saddle soap after every time they are used. When you have finished cleaning the leather and metal, always put the tack back in the tack room, where it belongs. Never leave it lying around on the ground. Someone could trip over it, or your pony could step on it.

When you put oil on the leather, try to brush it on evenly.

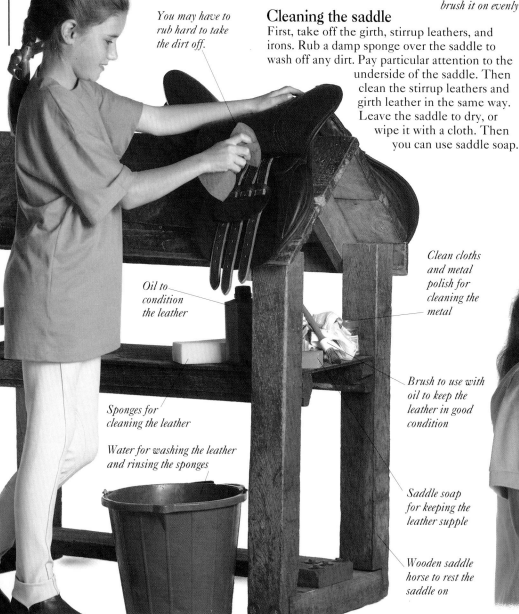

You may have to rub hard to take the dirt off.

Cleaning the saddle
First, take off the girth, stirrup leathers, and irons. Rub a damp sponge over the saddle to wash off any dirt. Pay particular attention to the underside of the saddle. Then clean the stirrup leathers and girth leather in the same way. Leave the saddle to dry, or wipe it with a cloth. Then you can use saddle soap.

Leather can break
Do not let the leather get too wet when you are washing the saddle or bridle. As leather dries, it becomes brittle, and it could eventually snap.

Using saddle soap
Once you have washed the leather, always apply saddle soap to keep the leather supple. Dip the soap into the water and rub it over the sponge. If you wet the sponge instead, you may find that you work up too much lather.

Oil to condition the leather

Clean cloths and metal polish for cleaning the metal

Sponges for cleaning the leather

Water for washing the leather and rinsing the sponges

Brush to use with oil to keep the leather in good condition

Saddle soap for keeping the leather supple

Wooden saddle horse to rest the saddle on

Keep a separate dry sponge to use with the saddle soap.

Storing the tack

Once the tack has been cleaned, it should be put away neatly in the tack room. Most tack rooms have special bridle hooks and saddle racks fitted to the walls. Sometimes these are labeled so that you know which pony's tack is which.

Bridles are usually hung up with the throatlatch crossed over the front, and the reins looped through it.

When you lift the saddle onto its rack, make sure you put it down gently. It should sit straight on its rack.

A saddle rack, which supports the saddle, is usually made of metal or wood.

Cleaning the bridle

It is best to take a bridle apart to clean it, but only if you know how to put it back together properly. Rinse the sponge and squeeze out the water. Then remove the dirt by wiping the sponge down each strap. When the bridle is dry, apply saddle soap with a clean sponge.

You can hang the bridle on a special hook while you are cleaning it. But be careful not to bang your head.

Wrap the sponge around the reins and pull it downward to remove the dirt.

Polishing the metal

Wash any mud off the stirrup irons, and wipe the bit with a damp sponge. Now rub metal polish over the irons and bit, and rub them with a soft cloth to make them gleam. When you have finished, rinse the bit in water so that your pony does not get polish in its mouth.

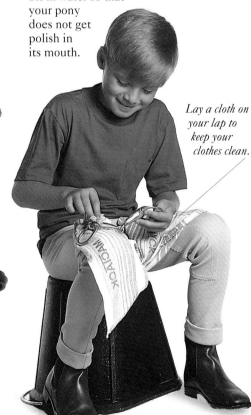

Lay a cloth on your lap to keep your clothes clean.

Catching and leading a pony

I F YOUR PONY is kept in a field, you will need to know how to catch it. When you go to collect your pony, it is a good idea to take a treat with you, to make the pony easier to catch. Never rush into a field noisily, or you may frighten all the ponies. Instead, approach quietly and calmly, so that your pony stands still to let you put the halter on. When you lead a pony out of the field, always use a lead rope, so if something startles the pony, you will be able to hold on. When you are leading, always walk through gates and doorways in a straight line so that the pony does not knock its sides. Finally, whenever you turn a pony out into a field, remember to shut the gate behind you.

Try not to startle your pony as you put the halter over its head.

Waiting your turn

If you are catching your pony with others, it is best to go into the field one or two at a time. This keeps the ponies calm. If they become excited, they may start to gallop around, so that you cannot catch them at all.

How to put on a halter

1 Walk toward your pony slowly from the front, so that it can see you. Hold the halter behind your back with one hand, and a treat in the other hand. Talk to the pony gently and say its name, then offer it the treat with your hand held out flat. As soon as the pony takes the treat, slip the free end of the lead rope around its neck.

2 While the pony is eating the treat, slip the noseband over its nose with both hands, until it is about halfway up the nose. Then reach under the pony's jaw with your right hand, and pass the halter over the top of the pony's head, behind the ears and fasten it.

Walk up to the pony with the halter behind you.

Most ponies do not need to be bribed with food, but every pony loves a treat.

How to tie a quick-release knot

1 First, slip the free end of the rope through the ring, and bend it like this. The other end of the rope is attached to the pony's halter.

The pony's halter is tied on to this end of the rope.

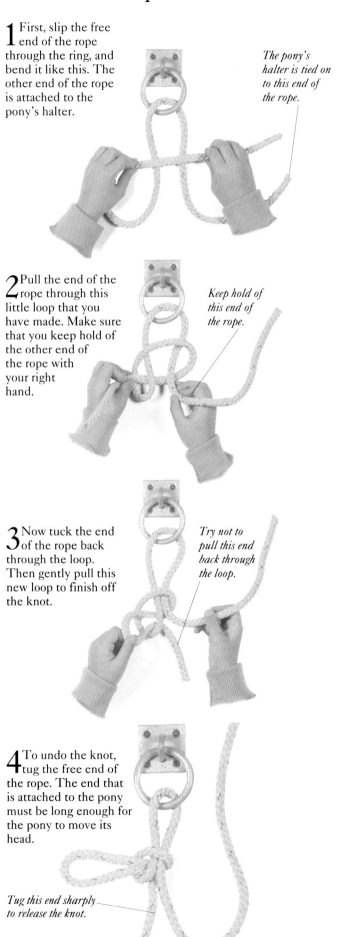

2 Pull the end of the rope through this little loop that you have made. Make sure that you keep hold of the other end of the rope with your right hand.

Keep hold of this end of the rope.

3 Buckle up the strap so that the halter fits loosely. The noseband should lie straight across the pony's nose. When you have finished, you can reward your pony with a pat or another treat.

Turning out

When you turn your pony out, lead it to the field in a halter. Never use a bridle in case the pony tries to run away with the bit in its mouth. Lead your pony through the gate. Then shut the gate behind you, and go a little way into the field. Turn the pony around to face the gate, and remove the halter.

3 Now tuck the end of the rope back through the loop. Then gently pull this new loop to finish off the knot.

Try not to pull this end back through the loop.

Tying up the pony

When you tie up a pony, use a quick-release knot. This is easy to undo in an emergency. You can also tie a piece of baling twine or string on to the tie-up ring first. Then, if your pony pulls hard while it is tied up, the string will break, and the pony will not hurt itself.

Some ponies can undo a knot by pulling the rope. If your pony does this, tuck the end through the loop.

4 To undo the knot, tug the free end of the rope. The end that is attached to the pony must be long enough for the pony to move its head.

Tug this end sharply to release the knot.

All about grooming

A PONY THAT LIVES in a stable should be groomed every day, to keep its skin healthy and its coat glossy. Ponies are always groomed when their coats are dry, because they are much easier to brush. Stabled ponies are given a quick grooming each morning, and a full grooming after a ride. A pony that lives in a field is not groomed as often because too much brushing would remove the oil that makes its coat waterproof. Grooming is hard work, but it is worth the effort. When you have finished, your pony's coat will have a healthy shine. Ponies enjoy being groomed, and may even nod off to sleep while you work.

2 Use the body brush to clean the coat. Start from behind the ears on the nearside, and brush in the direction of the hairs. Work down the neck and over the whole body, including the legs. Brush the other side in the same way. Every few strokes draw the curry comb through the brush to clean it. Finally, brush the pony's head gently.

Grooming a pastured pony

Before you ride a fieldkept pony, give it a quick groom with a dandy brush. This type of brush removes dried mud, which could rub under the tack and make the pony's skin sore. Next, tidy the mane and tail with a body brush, then use a hoof pick to clean the hooves. Finally, sponge the eyes, nose, and dock.

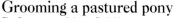

How to do a full grooming

1 Run your hand down the back of a foreleg, and pick up the hoof by holding the front. Scrape out any mud and stones with the hoof pick. Work from the heel toward the toe, and be gentle around the area called the frog. Clean each hoof in the same way. When you pick up a hind foot, run your hand down the back of the leg to the hock, then move it to the front. This helps protect your arm if the pony kicks out.

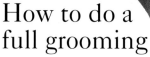

What you need

Here are some of the tools that you need for grooming. It is a good idea to keep them together in a box. Wash the brushes every so often, and rinse them thoroughly. Then leave them to dry.

Body brush for cleaning the coat

Hoof oil and brush for oiling the hooves

Sponge for the eyes, mouth, and nose, and another for the dock

Stable rubber to give the coat a final polish

Rubber curry comb

Metal curry comb for getting hairs and mud out of the body brush

Plastic curry comb for cleaning the brushes

Hoof pick for taking stones and mud out of the hooves

Dandy brush to remove dried mud and stable stains

As you are grooming, push with your body weight rather than just with your arm.

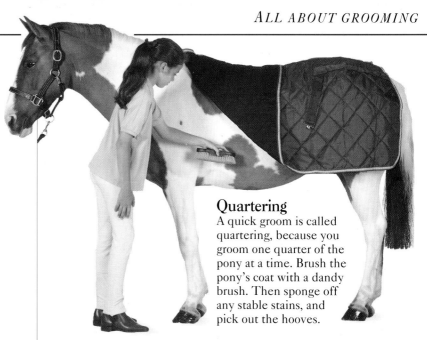

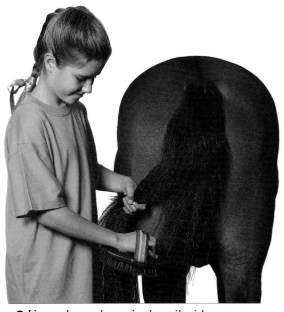

Quartering

A quick groom is called quartering, because you groom one quarter of the pony at a time. Brush the pony's coat with a dandy brush. Then sponge off any stable stains, and pick out the hooves.

3 Untangle any knots in the tail with your fingers. Then brush a few strands at a time with the body brush, so you won't pull out the hairs. Use a damp water brush to flatten the short hairs at the top of the tail. Next, brush the mane and forelock with the body brush. Use the water brush again to lay the mane flat against the neck.

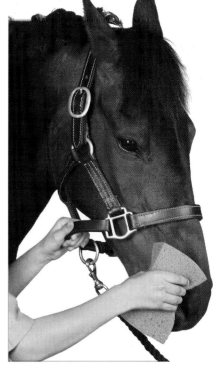

4 Keep one sponge for cleaning the dock, and dampen it before you use it. Hold the tail out to the side with one hand, then wipe the sponge under the tail with your other hand. Wash your hands and the sponge when you have finished.

5 Use a different sponge for the nose and eyes, and dampen it first. Gently wipe around the eyes, then rinse the sponge before you use it to clean the nose and mouth. Always wash the sponge afterward.

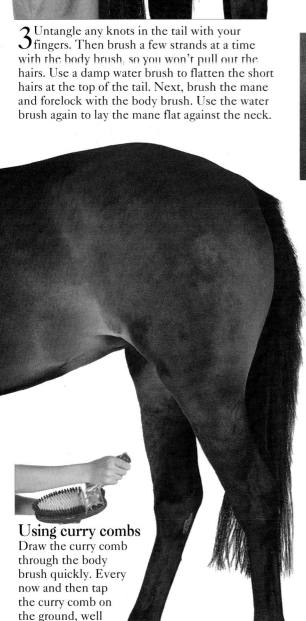

Please don't tickle

Some ponies are ticklish and may try to nip, or even kick you when you groom them, so be very careful.

6 When you have finished grooming with the body brush and sponges, dampen the stable rubber with some water. Scrunch it up and wipe it all over the coat in the direction of the hairs. This removes any dust that has settled, and makes the coat glossy.

Using curry combs

Draw the curry comb through the body brush quickly. Every now and then tap the curry comb on the ground, well away from the pony, to remove the dust.

Stable care

AS YOU BECOME more involved with riding, you will probably want to help out at the stables. You may be asked to muck out or sweep up the yard. Stable care is very important. Every riding school has to be kept clean and neat so that the ponies stay healthy. First thing each morning the ponies are given breakfast, then the stables are mucked out, and the yard is swept. Twice a day, before your pony's lunch and supper feeds, you should scoop out (muck out) its stable. The yard must be safe as well as neat, so check the latches on stable doors. Keep the feed shed door closed, just in case one of the ponies gets loose and wanders inside to help itself to a snack.

Sweeping the yard
To keep the yard neat, you need to sweep it after mucking out and at the end of each day. Once everything is in a pile, brush it on to a shovel, and lift it into the wheelbarrow.

What you need
Here are some of the tools that you need for keeping the stables and fields clean. Remember to put everything away after you have used it.

Broom for sweeping the yard

Four-pronged fork for lifting wet bedding and droppings

Shovel for picking up small bits of dirty bedding

Wheelbarrow for taking muck to the muck heap

Waterproof boots to keep your feet warm and dry

Rakes for gathering up wood shavings, leaves, and straw

Pitchfork for laying out the straw bedding

Scoop for picking up litter and droppings

Bedding
There are many kinds of bedding that you can put on the stable floor to make it comfortable. These include straw, peat, and even sand in hot countries. Here are some of the most common beddings.

Shredded newspaper

Wood shavings

Clean, dry straw

Fresh water
Fill the water troughs in each field with clean water every day. If there is no tap, use a bucket.

Neat and clean
You can pick up litter and droppings in the field with a small plastic scoop and rake.

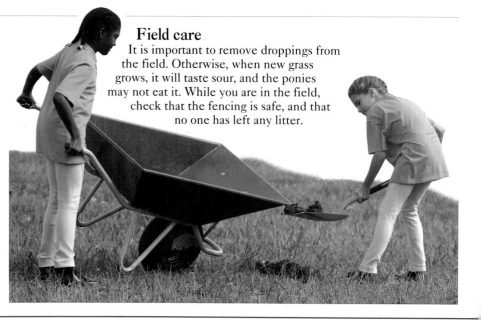

Field care
It is important to remove droppings from the field. Otherwise, when new grass grows, it will taste sour, and the ponies may not eat it. While you are in the field, check that the fencing is safe, and that no one has left any litter.

How to muck out

1 Use the pitchfork to lift up the dirty straw underneath the droppings, then tilt the fork so that the droppings fall into the wheelbarrow. Now toss any clean straw to the sides of the the stable so that you can reach the dirty straw underneath.

2 Put all the wet bedding into a pile, then lift it into the wheelbarrow with the fork. When the wheelbarrow is full, take it to the muck heap. You may need to ask a friend to help you. Stack up the muck heap neatly so that the dirty bedding rots down quickly.

Separate the sections of straw with a pitchfork, and spread the straw in a thick layer all over the floor.

3 Sweep up any remaining bedding into a pile, then lift it into the wheelbarrow with the shovel and take it to the muck heap. The stable floor should be clear now. Leave the stable to air for a while to let the floor dry before you lay down fresh bedding.

4 Collect enough fresh bedding to replace the wet bedding that you have removed, and lay it out with a pitchfork. The bed must be deep enough for the pony to stand on without scraping through to the floor. Remember to build up banks of bedding along the walls. This will help to stop the pony from becoming stuck if it lies down.

Quick clean up
A quick muck out should be done at least twice a day. You will need a fork and a plastic scoop, to remove droppings from the stable floor. Finally, neaten the bedding with the fork.

Food and feeding

IN THE WILD, a pony eats only grass. But ponies that we ride sometimes need other foods as well, to give them energy for the extra work they have to do. Ponies have small stomachs, so they are usually given three or four small meals throughout the day. Each pony has a special diet to suit its needs, with the correct amount and type of food. As you make friends with a pony, you will discover what kind of feeds it eats. All ponies need water, but they must never have too much immediately after exercise, as it can give them colic. Most ponies get all the nourishment they need in grass and hay, but some need extra vitamins and minerals. A vet can tell if a pony should be given supplements.

Good food

Hay is simply grass that has been cut and dried. Good hay smells sweet and is not dusty. It is fed to stabled ponies because they cannot graze outdoors. Pastured ponies are also given hay during the winter months, especially when the weather is bad and there is not enough grass to eat.

Pull the drawstring on the hay net before you hang it up.

Hanging up a hay net

Hay is hung up in a net so that the pony cannot tread on it or get its feet caught. To fill a hay net, separate the hay with a pitchfork, put it in the net, and pull the drawstring to close it. When you hang up the hay net, tie the string on to the net itself and use a quick-release knot (see p.45).

Dangerous plants

There are some plants that are poisonous if a pony eats them. Most ponies with enough grass in their field usually avoid these plants. But sometimes ponies out on a ride try to nibble at plants that are not good for them. So look out for yew, privet, acorns, deadly nightshade, bracken, and also ragwort, which looks like a yellow daisy. Do not let your pony eat these plants.

Yew often grows as a hedge, and can have berries.

Acorns fall from oak trees in the autumn.

Every pony likes to eat grass. But some ponies are greedy and eat too much, so they have to be put on a special diet.

The purple-flowered deadly nightshade grows in dark, damp places.

Apple

Carrot

Roots and fruits
Stabled ponies are often given chopped-up fruit and root vegetables to eat. These must always be cut lengthways so that the pony does not choke if it swallows them whole. You can give small pieces of apple or carrot to your pony as a treat.

Rutabaga

Salt lick
Some ponies need extra salt to replace the salt that they lose when they sweat. There may be a block of salt called a salt lick in your pony's stable.

Sugar beet

Sugar beet
A thin pony is given sugar beet or grain to fatten it up. The sugar beet must be soaked in plenty of water overnight first. If not, it can swell up in the pony's stomach and make it ill.

Linseed makes a pony's coat shine. But it is poisonous until it has been cooked.

Grain is like a kind of granola. It contains all sorts of good foods.

What a stabled pony eats
A pony that lives in a stable is given several different kinds of food to eat. These include oats, hay, and bran, plus some fruit and vegetables. Ask an adult to show you what kind of feed your pony eats. The feed is mixed up in a bucket, then taken to the pony's stable at feeding time. You can either tip the feed into the manger, or put it in a feed bowl on the stable floor.

This plastic feed scoop is for measuring each of the feeds.

Bran mash is a good food for ponies when they are tired or ill.

A feed bowl does not have any handles, so the pony cannot catch its leg.

Crushed or rolled barley is a good, filling winter feed.

Hay cubes or pellets are made up of condensed grass

Oats are given in small amounts because they can give a pony too much energy and make it excitable.

Chaff is simply chopped-up hay. It helps a pony digest its food.

Flaked maize is sometimes fed to ponies, but not often, because it can make them too energetic.

Your pony's health

A HEALTHY PONY is lively, with bright eyes and a glossy coat. But, just like you, your pony may not feel well all the time. Sometimes it may seem miserable and will not want to eat anything. Or its coat and eyes could become dull. If you notice that your pony's nose is runny, it has probably caught a cold. When a pony is ill, you must not ride it. While the pony is recovering, it is given hay and other low-energy foods to eat. It is usually best if the pony stays in its stable during this time, which is called "stall rest." If your pony is usually alert and happy, and you find that it is looking tired and unhappy, tell a responsible adult. The pony could be ill, and the vet may need to visit.

Fit and well
Healthy ponies love to roll in the field. So if your pony lies down and rolls in its field after exercising, this is a sign that it is happy, fit, and well.

A visit from the vet
Once a year, a vet needs to give your pony a vaccination. This is a type of injection to help prevent flu and tetanus. If your pony is ill, the vet may give it a series of injections or extra vitamins. A pony's teeth should also be checked by a horse dentist twice a year, in case they become too sharp and cut the pony's cheeks or make it difficult for the pony to eat.

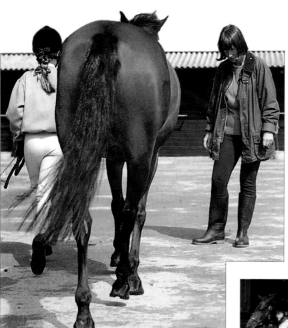

Trotting up
Sometimes a pony becomes lame. This means that it hops and nods its head as it is walking or trotting. The vet may ask you to "trot your pony in hand," up and down the yard. This means that you must lead your pony along so that the vet can see which leg is lame and why. You may be asked to trot your pony up several times, so that the vet can study the problem.

A pony that is not feeling well looks tired and dull.

Make sure that the loose end of the lead rope is not dangling down, and never wrap it around your hand.

🐎 Try not to tug
When you are trotting up, try not to pull at the pony's head as you are running along. If your pony is lazy, use a whip to hurry it up.

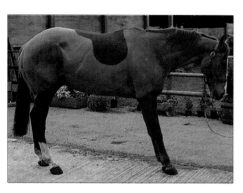

Common illnesses
If a pony has laminitis, its front feet are so sore that it stands oddly. The pony tries to relieve the pain by taking the weight mostly on its back legs, like this. Another common illness is colic, which is like a bad stomachache. Signs of colic include restlessness and fast breathing. If you see any of these signs, tell the adult in charge.

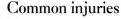

A visit from the farrier

A pony's hooves are made of horn, which grows like our fingernails. If your pony is working, its hooves may wear down and become sore. A farrier puts horseshoes on the pony's hooves to prevent this. The shoes need to be changed every few weeks as they wear down and the hooves grow longer. If your pony's hooves grow too long, the farrier will trim them.

Most ponies do not mind when the farrier replaces their shoes.

A vet is used to giving injections to ponies, so they do not usually hurt them.

You may want to ask the vet a few questions about your pony's illness.

Common injuries

Most ponies have a cut or a bruise at some time. They hurt themselves by treading on their own heels, and also by kicking each other. A pony may cut its leg on a sharp object. Every now and then, ponies knock their legs when they are jumping, so it is a good idea to use boots to prevent this. Make sure you learn how to put a boot on properly.

These boots wrap around the pony's legs to protect them.

How to bandage a leg

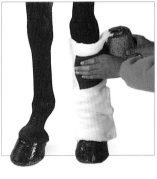

1 It takes practice to do this well, so ask an adult to help you. Wrap a piece of dressing around the leg. Do not overlap it on the tendons in case it causes pressure. Unroll the bandage, working downward. Keep the dressing smooth under the bandage.

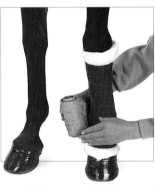

2 Overlap the edges of the bandage as you unroll it. At the fetlock joint do a "figure eight." Pass the bandage down at an angle under the joint, then back up at an angle. Try to keep the bandage even. It must be firm, but not tight.

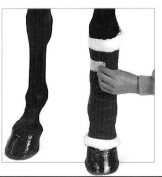

3 When you reach the top of the dressing, you should have unwound the whole bandage. Apply the self-adhesive tape or metal fasteners, then ask an adult to check that the bandage is on firmly and evenly.

Preparing for a show

GOING TO A SHOW can be very exciting, especially for the first time. If you go to a show, you and your pony need to look good. So make a list of what you have to do before you go. Brush your jacket and hat, polish your boots, and check that you have clean jodhpurs, shirt, tie, and gloves. A few days before the show, trim your pony's hair and "pull" its mane if you need to. The day before the show, clean the tack, polish the metal, and wash your pony if you need to. If you want to braid the pony's mane, wash it a few days earlier, so that it is easier to braid. If you are using a trailer to get to the show, check that your pony is not nervous about loading. If the pony is afraid, feed it inside the trailer a few times, until it becomes more relaxed.

Practice makes perfect
In the weeks leading up to the show, you can build up your confidence by practicing some jumping and games with your pony.

Washing the pony
You can wash your pony with a hose or a bucket and sponge. Wet the coat and rub in some shampoo, avoiding the eyes. Rinse out the soap with plenty of clean water. Scrape off any extra water with a sweat scraper, then dry the pony with a towel.

Trimming the hair
The long hairs on the heels are called "feathers." You may need to trim these before the show, with a mane comb and scissors. Run the comb upward through the feather, and snip off the hair that comes through the comb. Be careful not to snip the pony's heel with the scissors. On some breeds, the feathers should be left on. Before you start, find out if your pony's feathers should be trimmed or not.

Braiding the tail
This is difficult to do well, and it takes a great deal of practice. So if you would like your pony's tail to be braided for a show, ask someone experienced to do it for you. Once you have watched them a few times, you can try to do it yourself.

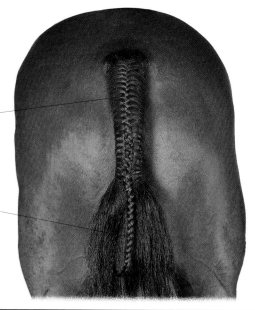

The whole tail is braided from the bottom of the dock.

The braid is continued to the very end without any more hair added to it. Then it is sewn up into a loop, like this.

Pulling the mane
Ask someone to help you to do this. Starting at the top of the neck, take a few of the longest hairs from the underside of the mane. Hold them firmly in one hand, and with the other hand, push the short hairs up to the roots with the comb. Now pull the long hairs down sharply to remove them. Do this as much as necessary to make the mane even.

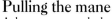

How to braid a mane

1 Dampen the mane first with a brush dipped in water. This will make it easier to braid. Divide the mane into sections. Put a rubber band on each section to keep it separate from the rest. Then braid all of the sections as neatly as possible, starting at the top of the mane. Finish off each braid by putting a rubber band on the bottom.

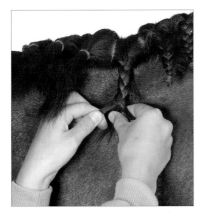

2 Now the braids need to be rolled up as neatly as possible. Take a braiding needle and thread, and pass the needle through the bottom of each braid twice, so that the thread is firmly attached. Roll each braid under, up to the crest of the mane, as tightly as you can, so that it looks like a knot. Hold the knot in place with one hand.

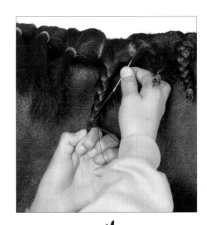

3 Still holding the braid in place, push the needle through the knot from the base. Wind the thread around to the right and pass the needle up through the middle. Then wind the thread around to the left and up through the middle again. Do this twice each way. To finish the knot, push the needle down through the middle, then snip off the needle and thread.

4 Braid the whole mane in the same way. Try not to be disappointed if it is not neat the first time. When you have finished, all the braids should be following the line of the pony's crest. If one or two of the knots are too low or too high, undo them and try again.

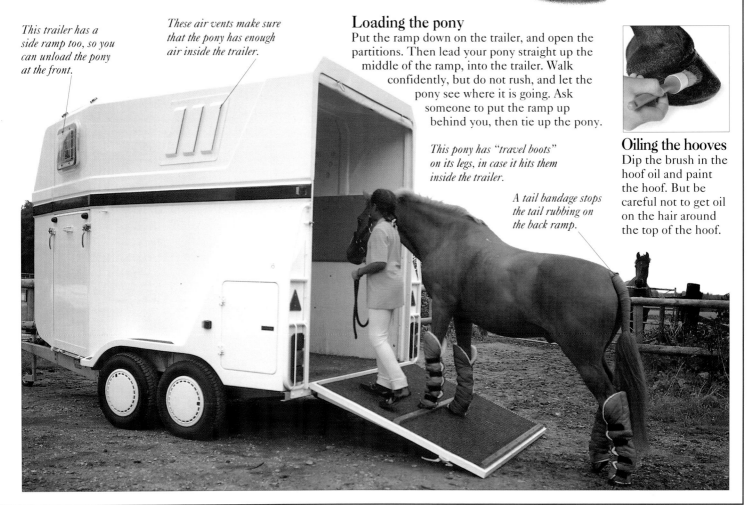

This trailer has a side ramp too, so you can unload the pony at the front.

These air vents make sure that the pony has enough air inside the trailer.

Loading the pony

Put the ramp down on the trailer, and open the partitions. Then lead your pony straight up the middle of the ramp, into the trailer. Walk confidently, but do not rush, and let the pony see where it is going. Ask someone to put the ramp up behind you, then tie up the pony.

This pony has "travel boots" on its legs, in case it hits them inside the trailer.

A tail bandage stops the tail rubbing on the back ramp.

Oiling the hooves

Dip the brush in the hoof oil and paint the hoof. But be careful not to get oil on the hair around the top of the hoof.

The day of the show

TAKING PART IN A SHOW is one of the most exciting things that a rider can do. There are all sorts of classes to enter, including jumping races. Sometimes the atmosphere is tense, especially if crowds of people are watching as well as taking part. If you are going to a show, make sure that you arrive early. It can take longer than you think to make your entries at the secretary's tent and collect your number. You also need to find out where and when your classes are to be held. However nervous you are, enjoy yourself. It is wonderful to win a prize, but even if you do not win, there will be plenty of other shows to enter. The most important thing is to have fun.

Winning a prize

If you win a prize, make sure that you thank your pony. Remember that the pony does most of the hard work.

Walking the course

Before a show jumping competition, it is useful to walk the course so that you know the route. Plan where you will need to turn, so that you can jump over the center of fences in a straight line.

Pony care at the show

When you are at the show, think of your pony's comfort before your own. Do not ride your pony all day long and exhaust it. Make sure that it rests between events, with its tack loosened or taken off. If the weather is hot, make sure that your pony is in the shade and give it plenty of water. Check every so often that your pony is happy and comfortable.

In this event, you have to lean out of the saddle to pick up a flag, then race to put it in the flag holder.

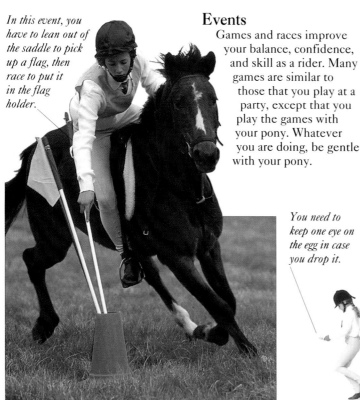

Events

Games and races improve your balance, confidence, and skill as a rider. Many games are similar to those that you play at a party, except that you play the games with your pony. Whatever you are doing, be gentle with your pony.

Egg and spoon race

In an egg and spoon race, you have to lead your pony with one hand, and hold an egg and spoon in the other. It is best to run alongside your pony, not in front of it, so that if you must stop suddenly, the pony will not bump into you.

You need to keep one eye on the egg in case you drop it.

If your pony is lazy, you may need to encourage it to hurry up.

Try to remember to look where you are going when you are jumping, instead of looking down at the jump.

Fence poles are usually painted white and one other color, such as red or yellow.

Show jumping

In show jumping, you have to jump over a course of fences. Your aim is to have a "clear round." This means that you must jump each fence without the pony refusing, running away, or knocking the fence down.

Your first show

At your first show, ask an experienced adult to help you decide which classes are suitable for you and your pony to enter. It is fun to try a little of everything so that you become a good "all-arounder." Try not to worry if you find some things more difficult than others. With practice, everything becomes easier.

After the show

Your pony will probably be as tired and as dirty as you are after the excitement of the show. You may need to wash the pony or brush off any dried sweat. At the end of the show, check that you do not leave anything behind, especially your crop or halter, which are easy to lose in the long grass.

Depending on the weather, you may need to put a blanket on your pony at the end of the day.

You can tie your pony to the trailer until you are ready to load.

A rider's world

THERE ARE all kinds of riding activities and sports for a rider to enjoy. Once you can ride well, and you feel confident on various horses and ponies, you may want to try an activity such as dressage, eventing, or polo. If you decide to take up riding as a career, you must be prepared to work very hard, and really enjoy what you do. With much good fortune, and many years of dedication, perhaps you could become a top-notch competition rider.

Eventing

In this sport, the horse and rider take part in three phases of competition. These are dressage, cross-country, and show jumping competitions. Eventing tests the skill of the rider and the ability and obedience of the horse.

This body protector is an important part of an event rider's gear.

Each event rider wears their own color scheme.

The crash helmet is usually covered with a colorful silk.

The horse is harnessed to a special racing cart called a "sulky."

The jockey carries a long riding whip.

This horse has been trained to trot very fast.

Each jockey wears special racing colors.

Harness races

Harness. or trotting, racing is a very popular sport in many parts of the world. It is like a chariot race, but the horse has to trot and must not canter. Some horses can trot as fast as a racehorse gallops. A harness race is usually about 1 mile (1.6 km) long.

Hunting

Many people join the hunt because they enjoy riding across open countryside. Some people who disapprove of hunting animals go "drag hunting" instead. For drag hunting, someone drags a scent around a course, for the hounds, and the hunt to follow.

The riders and horses are joined by a pack of dogs called hounds.

A hunt cap protects the rider's head.

The color of this hunt coat is called "hunt pink."

White breeches are for wearing with a red coat.

Hunting whip

These long "top" boots have blunt spurs on the heels.

The huntsman blows this horn to communicate with the hounds and the other riders.

Dressage

For dressage, the horse and rider have to perform special movements at set markers in the dressage arena. It takes many years of training to do this well.

For a dressage competition, the rider wears a formal tail coat and a top hat.

Show jumping

A show jumping course tests a rider's skill and a horse's jumping ability. The course usually includes several different kinds of fence. Some are double fences, and others are water jumps. The rider's aim is to achieve a "clear round" in the fastest time, without making any mistakes. Sometimes in a show-jumping competition, there are cross-country fences, like the one in this picture.

Polo

This is a very fast, exciting game that is played by two teams of riders on horseback. Each team tries to score as many goals as possible. The ponies that are trained to play this game can stop, start, turn, and sprint extremely quickly. The game is very tiring for these polo ponies, so each rider may have to ride several ponies during one game.

These gloves help the rider grip.

Helmet

Polo players wear long brown boots.

Polo sticks are made of bamboo.

Knee guards protect the rider's legs.

A polo ball is made of wood.

Western riding

The western style of riding comes from the United States, where cowboys and cowgirls ride in this way for working with cattle. Western riding is an enjoyable way of riding, especially if you spend many hours in the saddle.

The outfit includes a cowboy hat and leather chaps, which protect the rider's legs.

The stirrup leathers are long and the saddle is deep, to make it comfortable.

For Western riding, both reins are in one hand.

The stirrup leathers are very short for racing.

Racing

People enjoy watching horse racing all over the world. It is even more exciting for the jockeys and horses taking part in a race. There are three main types of race, which are flat racing, hurdling, and steeplechasing. Flat racing is very fast and has no jumps, and steeplechasing is a longer race, which includes large, bushy fences. This picture shows a flat race.

Becoming involved

I F YOU REALLY enjoy being with ponies, the best way to become more involved is to help out at a riding stable after school or on the weekends. You could also join a pony club, which has lessons, camps, and outings where you can learn more about horses and ponies. If you would like to work with horses, there are courses you can take to give you the skills you will need. But remember, no amount of coursework is better than years of hard work in the stables.

Riding vacations

Vacations that involve riding range from a day's trek to a week or more at a riding center, where you are given a pony to look after and ride for the whole vacation. If you are a member of the Pony Club, you can go away to "camp," and stay in cabins, tents, or houses.

Grooming as a career can be very rewarding, especially as you make friends with the horses and ponies in your care.

Working with horses

There are several jobs that include working with horses, including grooming, teaching, and farrier work. Each of these jobs involves long hours and hard work. So before you decide which kind of work you would like best, you need to spend as much time as possible working at a stable or a riding school, to find out exactly what is involved.

Being a farrier

Becoming a farrier takes many years of training, and it is very hard work.

Working as a groom

For some grooming jobs you need to be able to ride, but not always. The important thing is that you know how to care for horses and ponies.

Being an instructor

To be an instructor, you must train for several years, improve your riding skills and horse knowledge, and take teaching exams.

Major events

Here are some big riding events, such as shows, races, and Grand Prix that you may want to go to during the year.

APRIL
MARYLAND HUNT CUP – Steeplechase, Glyndon, MD
ROLEX KENTUCKY THREE-DAY EVENT – Combined training, Lexington, KY
$100,000 BUDWEISER AMERICAN INVITATIONAL – Show jumping, Tampa, FL
MAY
ESSEX THREE-DAY EVENT – Combined training, Gladstone, NJ
KENTUCKY DERBY – Thoroughbred race, Louisville, KY
JUNE
U.S. EQUESTRIAN TEAM FESTIVAL OF CHAMPIONS – Dressage, show jumping and driving, Gladstone, NJ
JULY
INTERNATIONAL ARABIAN HORSE ASSOC. YOUTH NATIONAL – Breed show, Oklahoma City, OK
THE TEVIS CUP – 100-mile endurance ride, Auburn, CA
THE WORLD PAINT SHOW – Breed show, Fort Worth, TX
AUGUST
AMERICAN SADDLEBRED WORLD GRAND CHAMPIONSHIPS – Breed show, Louisville, KY

NORTH AMERICAN YOUNG RIDERS CHAMPIONSHIPS – Dressage, show jumping, combined training, Wadsworth, IL
SEPTEMBER
THE LITTLE BROWN JUG – Pacing race, Delaware, OH
$85,000 CADILLAC GOLD CUP – Show jumping, Devon, PA
OCTOBER
GLADSTONE FALL DRIVING EVENT – Carriage driving, Gladstone, NJ
INTERNATIONAL GOLD CUP – Steeplechase, The Plains, VA
RADNOR INTERNATIONAL THREE-DAY EVENT – Combined traiing, Malvern, PA

U.S. ARABIAN NATIONAL – Breed show, Albuquerque, NM (odd years), Louisville, KY (even years)
U.S. OPEN POLO CHAMPIONSHIPS – Indio, CA
NOVEMBER
THE AMERICAN ROYAL – Show and rodeo, Kansas City, MO
THE NATIONAL HORSE SHOW – East Rutherford, NJ
RAM TAP THREE-DAY EVENT – Combined training, Fresno, CA
DECEMBER
NATIONAL CUTTING HORSE WORLD CHAMPIONSHIP FUTURITY – Forth Worth, TX

Useful addresses

Here are addresses for some groups and associations you might want to join, visit, or write to for information.

American Horse Protection Association
1000 29th St., NW., #T-100
Washington, DC 20007
(202) 965-0500

American Horse Shows Association
220 E. 42nd St., Suite 409
New York, NY 10017-5809
(212) 972-2472

American Horse Council
1700 K St., NW, Suite 300
Washington, DC 20006
(202) 296-4031

American Riding Instructor Certification Program
P.O. Box 282
Alton Bay, NH 03810
(603) 875-4000

CHA/Association for Horsemanship Safety and Education
P.O. Box 188
Lawrence, MI 49064
(616) 674-8074

Horsemanship Safety Association
120 Ohio Ave.
Madison, WI 53704-5417
(608) 244-8547

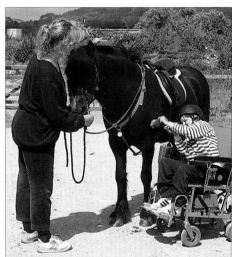

Kentucky Horse Park
4089 Iron Works Pike
Lexington, KY 40511
(606) 233-4303

National 4-H Council
7100 Connecticut Ave.
Chevy Chase, MD 20815
(301) 961-2945

North American Riding for the Handicapped Association
P.O. Box 33150
Denver, CO 80233
(303) 452-1212

United States Pony Clubs
4071 Iron Works Pike
Lexington, KY 40511
(606) 254-7669

Glossary

There are lots of interesting riding words and expressions. If you learn some of the words on these pages, you will find them useful during your riding lessons.

Hindquarters

A

AIDS The signals that a rider uses for communicating with a pony. For example, the hands, legs, and voice.

ARENA An enclosed area for training and exercising ponies with a good surface that does not become too hard or too muddy in bad weather.

B

BALK When a pony is stubborn and refuses to move in the right direction.

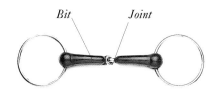

Bit   *Joint*

BARS The two areas inside a pony's mouth, one on either side, where there are no teeth. The bit is placed across these bars.

BIT A piece of tack attached to the reins that fits across the bars in a pony's mouth.

BODY BRUSH A soft, short-haired brush that you use for cleaning a pony's coat.

BOMB PROOF A pony that is not easily frightened, which is ideal for beginners.

BRIDLE A piece of tack that goes on the pony's head for riding. It is made up of the headstall, browband, throatlatch, cheek pieces, noseband, reins, and bit.

BROWBAND The part of the bridle that fits around a pony's forehead.

C

CANTLE The highest part of a saddle, at the back.

CAST When a pony can not get up from a lying down position.

CAVALETTI Wooden poles 10ft (3m) long, that are supported on crossbars for jumping.

CAVESSON NOSEBAND The simplest type of noseband. A cavesson is also a type of halter that has a ring on the noseband for attaching a lunge line to.

CHANGING REIN Changing the pony's direction from the "left rein" to the "right rein" in an arena.

CLEAR ROUND Jumping each fence in a competition without the pony knocking the fence down, refusing, or running out.

COLIC A bad stomachache.

CONFORMATION The overall shape of a pony, and the way that it is put together.

CONTACT The link between the rider's hands and a pony's mouth through the reins.

CORONET A sensitive area around the top of the hoof where it joins the leg.

CREST A ridge on the top of the neck.

CURRY COMBS Metal curry combs are used to remove hairs and oil from a body brush. Plastic and rubber curry combs are used like a dandy brush to remove mud and hair from a pony's coat.

D

DANDY BRUSH A medium-hard brush with long bristles for removing mud from a pony's coat.

DISMOUNT To get off a pony.

DOCK The bony part at the top of a pony's tail.

DOUBLE BRIDLE A bridle with two bits in the pony's mouth (a "curb" and a "bridoon"), used for highly trained ponies taking part in dressage and showing classes.

DRESSAGE A sport in which a pony or horse is trained to perform special movements in a particular way.

E

EGGBUTT A type of joint on a bit that stops the corners of the pony's mouth from being pinched between the rings and the mouthpiece of a bit.

ELBOW The bony point at the back of a pony's forearm.

ERGOT A hard (but not bony) lump that sticks out from the back of the fetlock joint. It is usually hidden under the feathers.

EVENTER A horse that is trained for show jumping, dressage, and cross-country riding.

F

FARRIER A trained person who takes care of a pony's hooves and fits new shoes.

FEATHERS The long hairs that grow at the back of the fetlock joints.

FETLOCK JOINTS The joints that stick out above the pony's hooves.

FIGURE EIGHT A movement that you make in the shape of the number eight.

FLANKS The pony's sides, between the ribs and the back legs.

FLEABITTEN GRAY A white pony with a freckled coat.

FLEHMEN When a pony curls its lip in response to an unusual smell or taste.

FOAL A newborn pony (up to 12 months).

FORELEG A pony's front leg.

FORELOCK The part of the mane that lies between the ears and falls onto the forehead.

FORWARD SEAT The riding position for jumping or galloping when the stirrups are shortened to help balance. The faster the pace, the shorter the stirrups need to be.

FROG The tough, elastic material in the center of the pony's sole, under the hoof.

G

GAIT A pony's pace, such as walking, trotting, and cantering.

GELDING A castrated male pony.

GIRTH A strap placed around the pony's belly to keep the saddle in position.

GRAZING The paddock or field where a pony is turned out to graze.

GROOMING Brushing a pony's coat to keep its skin clean, shiny, and healthy, and the pony comfortable.

GYMKHANA A riding event with all sorts of games and races that riders and their ponies can take part in.

H

HALTER A headstall, noseband, and throatlatch for catching, tying up, and leading a pony or horse.

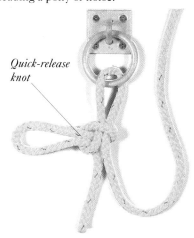

Quick-release knot

HANDS A unit of measurement that equals about 4 in (10 cm), used for determining a pony's height.

HEADSTALL The part of the bridle or halter that lies behind a pony's ears.

HINDQUARTERS The back end of a pony, including the hind (back) legs.

HOCK The joint on a pony's hindleg.

I

INSIDE HAND OR LEG The rider's hand or leg that is on the inside when he or she is riding in a circle.

L

LAME When a pony has an ailment or injury that makes it painful to move normally.

LAMINITIS Sore hooves (also called "fever of the hooves"). It is usually caused by overeating.

LEAD LEG The front leg that reaches farthest forward when a pony is cantering

LEAD OFF The moment that a pony's pace changes from trot to canter.

LEAD RIDER The rider at the front.

LEFT HAND TO LEFT HAND When two riders pass each other with their left hands and the ponies' left sides facing.

LEG UP When someone helps a rider spring up, onto a pony.

LOADING Leading a pony into a trailer.

LOOSE RING A type of snaffle bit, where the bit rings are not fixed to the mouthpiece but can be pulled through it.

LUNGEING When a pony is being trained on a lunge line attached to a cavesson. The trainer stands on the ground and works the pony around in a circle, using a lunge whip to keep it going forward.

M

MANGER A fixed trough (or box) in a stable that a pony can feed from.

MARE a female pony that is four or more years old.

MOUNTING BLOCK A low block of steps for a rider to stand on for mounting.

MUZZLE A pony's nose, lips, and chin.

N

NEARSIDE The left side of a pony (when you look from the back toward the front).

NECK STRAP A strap that is placed around the pony's neck for a beginner to hold on to for extra safety.

NEW ZEALAND BLANKET Waterproof canvas blanket for a pony that lives outside.

NOSEBAND The part of the bridle or halter that lies around the pony's nose. The most simple one is a cavesson noseband.

O

OFFSIDE The right side of a pony (looking from the back of a pony toward the front).

OUTSIDE HAND OR LEG The hand or leg that is on the outside when a rider is moving in a circle.

P

PASTERN The part of a pony's leg between the fetlock and the hoof.

PELHAM A type of bit with two reins, that works in a similar way to a double bridle.

PICKING OUT Using a hoof pick to remove mud and stones from the hooves.

PINTO A pony's coat that is patched with white and any color.

POLL The part of the head between the ears.

POMMEL The raised part at the front of a saddle.

PULLING Removing hairs from the mane and tail to make them neater.

Q

QUARTERING A quick groom to remove stable stains and tidy up a pony.

Safety stirrups

QUICK-RELEASE KNOT A knot that is secure, but quick and easy to undo in an emergency.

R

REARING When a pony rises up on its back legs.

REFUSAL When a pony stops in front of a fence instead of jumping over it.

RIGHT HAND TO RIGHT HAND When two riders pass each other with their right hands and the ponies' right sides facing.

ROLLER A strap fastened around a pony's belly to keep a blanket in place.

RUB RAG A type of cloth that you use after grooming to remove dust from a pony's coat.

RUNNING UP THE STIRRUPS Sliding the stirrup irons to the top of the leathers.

RUN-OUT Running to the side of a fence instead of jumping over it.

Quartering

S

SADDLE HORSE A wooden or metal frame to put a saddle on for cleaning.

SADDLE PAD A soft pad that is put under the saddle to absorb sweat and protect the pony's back.

SADDLE SORES Sores that can form on a pony's back if its saddle is dirty or fits badly.

SCHOOL MOVEMENTS Set exercises that the pony and rider must perform accurately at set markers in the arena.

SEAT How a rider sits on a pony. If you have a "good seat," it means that you are secure on your pony. A "deep seat" comes with years of experience.

SHYING When a pony swerves sideways away from an object or a noise.

SNAFFLE BITS The most common group of bits, which have rings on both sides of the mouthpiece.

SOUND A pony that is not lame.

STABLE STAINS Dirt and marks that have dried on a pony's coat after it has spent the night in a stable, lying on droppings.

STABLED PONY A pony that spends most of its time in a stable rather than in a pasture.

STALLION A male pony used for breeding.

STALL REST When a pony is kept in its stable to rest while it recovers from an illness.

STIRRUP LIGHTS Battery-operated lights that attach to stirrups for use at night.

STIRRUPS Two metal loops that are attached to the saddle by stirrup leathers, for a rider to put his or her feet in.

SUSPENSION (MOMENT OF) When all four legs are off the ground for an instant

during the gallop.

SWEAT SCRAPER A piece of equipment that you use to remove excess water after washing a pony's coat.

T

TACK A general term for the saddle, bridle, and other equipment needed to ride a pony.

TACKING UP Putting on the tack.

THROATLATCH The strap attached to the headstall, which fastens loosely under the pony's jaw.

THROWING A SHOE When a pony loses one of its shoes by accident.

TRAIL RIDING Riding out in the open countryside.

TRANSITION A change of gait.

TREE The frame inside a saddle.

TROTTING UP When you run up and down with a pony in hand so that someone can watch its movement, usually to see if it is lame.

TROUGH (WATER) A large basin, sometimes automatic, which the pony can drink from.

TURN OUT To put a stabled pony out in a pasture or arena for rest or exercise.

U

UNSOUND A lame pony.

W

WATER BRUSH A brush that you use to dampen the mane and tail, remove stable stains, and wash muddy hooves.

WEAVING A nervous habit (usually as a result of boredom), when a pony rocks from side to side in its stall.

WESTERN RIDING A style of riding in which the reins are held in one hand, the stirrups are long, and the saddle is very deep. This style of riding was first used by cowboys who spent many hours in the saddle.

WITHERS The base of the pony's neck, where it joins the body above the shoulders.

Y

YEARLING A pony that is one year old.

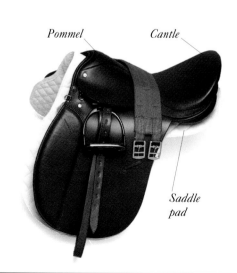
Pommel   *Cantle*

Saddle pad

Index

Marissa and Harold   Nathalie and Sunny   Phillippa and Mr Phillibus   Christophe and Pappy

Acknowledgments

Dorling Kindersley would like to thank the following people (and ponies) for their help in the production of this book:

Nereide and John Goodman, and the staff of Wellington Riding, for their patience and enthusiasm, especially Robert Pickles, Phillippa Muir, Louise Watts, Paula Dawkins, Vicky Capp, and Bonnie Dickason. Also, Sir Jellico, the grey (owned by Nereide Goodman and Sue Mears); Sunny (owned by Caroline Phillips and Wellington Riding); Harold, Pappy, and Mr Phillibus (owned by Wellington Riding). For the props, we are grateful to Nicholas Ward, Hydrophane Laboratories, Ickleford, for hats, gloves, and other equipment; Ian Compton, Calcutts, Sutton Scotney, for riding jackets; Sue Kayne, Lambourn, Newbury, for the trailer; Michael Kent, Tally Ho (UK) Ltd., Whitchurch, for jodhpurs; British Home Stores for sweaters; and Wellington Riding for various pieces of equipment; Robert Pickles, Phillippa Muir, Louise Watts, Nereide Goodman, Christiane Gunzi,

and Vicky Capp for modelling; Louise Pritchard, Gillian Cooling, Claire Bampton, and Michelle Lynch, for editorial assistance; Susan St. Louis for design assistance: Jane Turton for help during photography sessions; Pete Serjeant for the illustration p.25; and Pru Davies for allowing us to photograph Merry Dock the Hobbit p.52*t*).

The author wishes to thank:
Gig Lees for looking after my horses for many years, which has enabled her to become an integral part of this project. Gig has been been invaluable at every stage of the book's production. My thanks are also owed to all the two- and four-legged people who have taken me from the earliest stages to the completion of this book.

Picture credits
Allsport/Gary M. Prior: 7*br*; **Barn Owl Associates:** 7*bl*; 30*b*; **Robert Harding Picture Library:** 60*bl*; **Kit Houghton:** 30*tr*; 31; 58*tc*, bl; 59*br*
Bob Langrish: 4; 7*tr*, *cra, ca, cr*; 8*tr*; 9*cla, cb, bc*; 10*br, bc*; 11*tl, tc, tr, cla, ca, cra, cr, clb, cb, crb, bc, bl, br*; 13*br*; 20*b*; 22-3*tc*; 25*cl*; 27*t, c*; 28*c*; 29; 30*cl*; 32-3*tc*; 33*cl*; 34*cl*; 35*bc*; 45*cl, bl*; 52*bl*; 53*tr*; 54*c*; 56*bl*; 57*tl, b*; 59*tl, tr, cl, cr*; 60*tl, tr*; 61; 62*tr*; **Floyd Sayers:** 44*cl*.

Additional DK photography: Peter Chadwick, Dave King, Andrew McRobb, Stephen Oliver, Tim Ridley, Jerry Young.

key: *b* bottom, *c* centre, *l* left, *r* right *t* top